This Is Not A Book

The bookshelves are full of them. Book after book talking about the importance of creativity, imagination, and the need for innovation. This is not one of those books.

Yes, these pages are about unleashing your imagination, achieving a creative mindset, and harnessing the power of innovative thinking. But this is not your typical book. Why? Because I think you've read enough books that tell you why innovation is important. They're great in the moment and then end up sitting on your shelves collecting dust.

This is a playbook. This is the "how."

A playbook is a coach's guide. In football and many other sports, a playbook includes the strategies and descriptions of all the plays. Coaches and players often memorize the playbook at the start of the season and then add to it as they encounter new situations on the field.

In the game of disruptive thinking, a playbook is your personal guide. You can open it up to any segment, any page, any visual, and apply that tool to your situation. A playbook for both sports and disruptive thinking is a living, breathing resource that you continually update, edit, and review.

This is your playbook for thinking sideways, acting sideways, and believing sideways, and ultimately for achieving sideways results. The tools here will get you into the right attitude and mindset, and give you specific exercises that you can use to unleash new ideas right now.

That is how I approached *Think Sideways: A Game-Changing Playbook for Disruptive Thinking*. The words on the page, visuals between the text, the QR codes and links to online resources, and webisodes of *imagi-NATION™: disruptive innovators road tour* will be added to as new ideas and resources are uncovered—by you! You will take notes and customize the exercises to meet your specific needs. Awesome! Most authors would shudder at the idea of a reader editing their book, but I say go for it! (I'm not so much an "author" anyway. I'm more of a lover of disruption and sideways thinking.)

This playbook is a culmination of my years of entrepreneurial know-how, corporate experience, and personal knowledge. Years that have taught me that doing things the same as everyone else does gets you to the same place everyone else is going. But doing things your own way puts you on your own path.

Enjoy!

There are so many moments when this playbook will serve you:

You may be stuck in a mental rut . . . **No problem! Just whip it open to any tool and get unstuck.**

You may be sitting at the kitchen table with that gnawing feeling that your big idea is out there somewhere calling out to you . . . **Get going! Any tool in this book will help guide you to it.**

You may be frustrated because you are that sideways thinker in a sea of sameness . . . **Rock on! Use these tools to engage the crowd.**

You may be yearning to disrupt the status quo that bogs you down . . .**Tackle it! You can't help but disrupt with these tools.**

You may know that what you are working on is going to fall flat but can't figure out what to do . . . **No worries! We've got some tools to help you shake things up.**

You may be getting a group of sideways thinkers together for an ideation session . . . **Awesome! Use any of the tools to craft a fruitful day.**

You can read this playbook cover-to-cover, frontwards or backwards, or you can skip from segment to segment.

There is no one right way to immerse yourself in sideways thinking. What I can tell you is that once you delve in, you'll want to take notes as the innovative ideas and fresh thinking start flooding in. There are thought bubbles throughout the book for you to do just that. They are for you to write down any and all sideways questions and ideas.

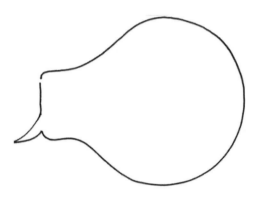

The bite-sized exercises spread throughout the playbook are for you to literally photocopy and place anywhere that helps you—on your desk, refrigerator, back door.

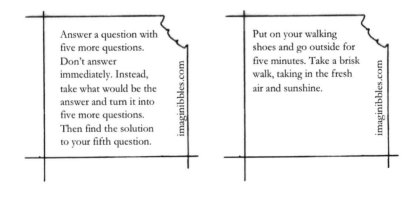

Answer a question with five more questions. Don't answer immediately. Instead, take what would be the answer and turn it into five more questions. Then find the solution to your fifth question.

imaginibbles.com

Put on your walking shoes and go outside for five minutes. Take a brisk walk, taking in the fresh air and sunshine.

imaginibbles.com

You can also download them and many other resources on the website by following the many QR Codes in this playbook. The QR Codes take you to a password protected area that has every worksheet, imagi-NATION™ episode, and more. You'll want to check back because we'll add more as we discover it.

The password is "think".

imaginibbles.com/think-sideways-playbook/

The only problem with this playbook is, with all the ideas that will spring forth, even all those blank spaces might not be enough room! Once you start engaging you can't help but let the ideas flood in. You'll have made a crack in the dam, and sooner or later your sideways mind won't be able to hold back. Always keep a pen handy because you're going to need it. As the segment on Popcorn says, sideways thinkers capture all ideas without judgment or analysis. If an idea of any kind—a hint of an idea, a percolating thought, an image, a sketch of a start of an idea, a question—comes to you, get it down.

My hope is that over time and many reads, you'll fill all the blank spaces in this book with thoughts, and that ultimately one of those thoughts turns into your DREAM BIG path in life, and that big dream makes a big dent in the world.

  Get your mind and your pen ready. Forecast says high probability of mind-blowing ideas and afternoon innovation showers.

If I'm just getting started, how should I use this playbook?

Pick one sideways mindset from the segment on SIDEWAYS ATTITUDES AND ACTIONS and one exercise from the SIDEWAYS EXERCISES to do daily. It's the combination that produces extreme sideways results. Each day, thumb through and pick two. You might decide to focus on LEAN IN and SMASH one day, and ANTENNAS UP and SPONTANEOUS COLLABORATION on the next. You'll notice places in the playbook that say "jump to…" The concept on one page links to another in some way, so get ready to take a journey.

You can open this playbook to any page and harness the exercises and ideas on that page, so do what works for you. If it gets you to disruptive thinking, I don't care how you do it.

If you have a group of sideways thinkers, and want to talk to Tamara about some of the lessons, experiences, and ideas in this playbook, reach out. We will set up a 30-minute video or conference call to talk about all things sideways.
team@imaginibbles.com

Think Sideways

a game-changing playbook for disruptive thinking

by Tamara Kleinberg

aka Chief Imaginator @ imaginibbles

ISBN: 978-0-9852447-0-5

Generally Speaking, Inc. Publishing
Printed in U.S.A.

Book cover by Astrid Koch
Innovation super heroes artwork by Michelle Kondrich
Editorial assistance by Jed Heneberry
Research and assistance by Kelly O'Connell

This book is dedicated to all of you that have ever been told you are doing it wrong...

... and of course, my amazing family, friends, and dog.

"Impossible is just a big word thrown around by small men who find it easier to live in the world they've been given than to explore the power they have to change it. Impossible is not a fact. It's an opinion. Impossible is not a declaration. It's a dare. Impossible is potential. Impossible is temporary. Impossible is nothing."
— Muhammad Ali

WHAT IS SIDE WAYS THINKING?

www.imaginibbles.com/think-sideways-playbook/

Thinking Sideways is NOT:

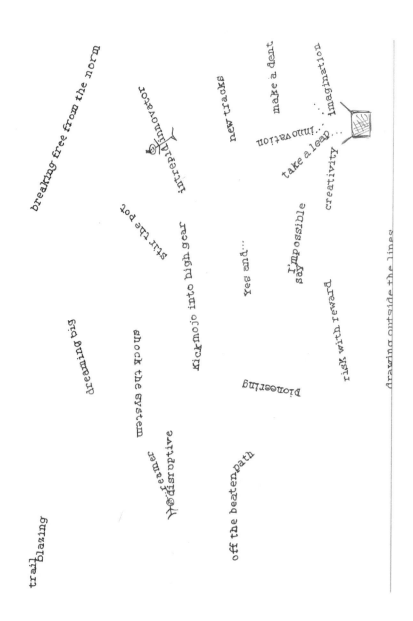

Thinking Sideways IS:

breaking free from the norm

intrepid innovator

new tracks

make a dent

innovation...

imagination

take a leap...

creativity

stir the pot

Kickmojo into high gear

yes and...

i'mpossible say

risk with reward

drawing outside the lines

dreaming big

shock the system

pioneering

dreamer @ disruptive

off the beaten path

trailblazing

a game-changing playbook for disruptive thinking

Thinking Sideways feeds your need to rebel against the status quo and put a dent in life-as-usual. This is your chance to be disruptive.

  DISRUPTION: cause turmoil; destroy normal continuance of unity; disrupt a connection.

I don't need to tell you that now, more than ever, we need sideways thinkers like you. We need more dents in the status quo, more disruptions of business-as-usual, and more people realizing their dreams, large and small.

Thinking Sideways is about stepping off the beaten path and carving your own road.

Life is full of sideways thinkers who have disrupted life-as-usual. You know who they are. They are usually labeled the rebels, the mavericks, the pioneers. They are all of these things and more.

They are seen in businesses like Square Inc. (challenged complicated and expensive payment options by delivering a simple, minimal-fee app anyone can use), Zappos (focused on happiness and delivered customer satisfaction as if they were a brick and mortar store, totally altering our expectations of online shopping), and Massage Envy (turned a high-end treat, spa services, into a mainstream subscription business, making massages and facials part of anyone's daily routine), and in people like Perry Chen, Yancey Strickler, and Charles Adler (founders of Kickstarter.com, an online crowdfunding website for creative projects that ignores traditional investing protocols), Quentin Tarantino (continually challenging how movie stories are told, like telling it backwards and parallel in *Pulp Fiction*), and Sara Blakely of Spanx (pursuing an ah-ha moment and turning cutoff stockings into a body-forming mega-business).

They are the innovative business owners in our communities, like Emma from The Shoppe (bucking the pretty little cupcake trend and creating a place where anyone can go and feel like a kid again) or Dan from Solid State Depot (a community dedicated to innovation and turning wild ideas into reality).

They are people like you and me who aren't satisfied with business as usual—and they (you) are needed now more than ever.

Let's face it—we live in crazy times. I'm, how do you say, not as young as I used to be. I'm not exactly old either, but I do remember when cell phones were the size of a loaf of bread, microwave cooking was all the rage, and the video game *Pong* was totally radical.

Funny, it wasn't that long ago. It didn't take generations for a cell phone to go from a 10-pound behemoth to fitting a Space Shuttle's worth of computing power into the palm of your hand. We live in times of lightning-fast change, and the truth is that it will probably never slow down. I think that's good. With constant change comes constant opportunity. There will always be something new to learn, something interesting to try, and something exciting to pursue. Like my experience as a kid changing schools every few years, when change comes about, so does the opportunity to chart a new path.

Now go make a big @#* dent!

BUT I DON'T OWN FUNKY EYEWEAR!
DEBUNKING THE MYTHS

www.imaginibbles.com/think-sideways-playbook/

There are a lot of myths when it comes to thinking sideways. Those myths keep sideways thinking at bay. They hold you back from reaching your creative potential because they perpetuate an incorrect set of rules that exclude instead of include. You have probably believed some of these in the past and may even hold on to a few right now. Let's shatter those myths and create a clear path for you to think sideways.

Myth #1: You have to be a hip, glasses-wearing freelancer with a blue streak in your hair to be creative.

Yes, that guy is probably creative—but so are you. Creativity isn't just for the elite few who know all the new dive bars. It's for everyone, and it's inside all of us. The proof is in your life. If you've ever gone to the theater and enjoyed a great movie totally based in a fantasy world, like *Avatar, Harry Potter*, or *Lord of the Rings*, then you are creative. The funny part is that we often abdicate creativity to others. In conversations we look to them instead of ourselves for sideways thinking. We shut up and let them do their magic. What if you expected the same from yourself? Because you have just as many good ideas as they do.

If we ever meet, you'll find that, while I'm considered an innovation and entrepreneurial thought leader, in no way do I fit the stereotype, and I'm guessing you don't either. If you look up a picture of any of your favorite sideways thinkers, I'm betting that most of them don't fit the stereotype either.

25

  Who is ur favorite sideways think-er? Share w/other imaginators on fb: http://ow.ly/8vcuk

Myth #2: Creativity is about painting a beautiful piece of artwork or being able to dance effortlessly.

Creativity is, in fact, not about output at all—it's about the process. Yes, painting is a creative process, but so is creative problem solving, looking for new opportunities and adapting to the unknown. If you focus on being creative in the process, then the output will always be creative. I get really frustrated with books about unleashing creativity that only tell you to learn to play an instrument or take a class in watercolor. I'd encourage you to do both, but creativity is so much more than that. First, that kind of creativity leaves out the two other pieces in the puzzle: imagination and innovation. Second, it leaves out the goal—thinking sideways. The goal should be about thinking sideways every day, not just when you are engaging in "creative" activities. So expand your definition of creativity beyond how to draw and think of it as a way of being (note: sideways attitudes and actions will show you how to do just that).

a game-changing playbook for disruptive thinking

Myth #3: Being creative is hard work.

Not really! In fact, it can be quite easy if you allow it to be. The problem is that we shut down our sideways thinking day-to-day, and then expect it to kick into gear in a pinch. No warm up, no exercises, and it fails. So we think it's hard work. The truth is that the sideways thinking mind is a lot like the muscles in your body. It needs regular exercise and nutritious fuel to get stronger. If you wanted to get fit and strengthen your muscles, you wouldn't go to the gym once a year and expect results. No, you would set that alarm clock, get up, and go to the gym five days a week. In 60 minutes, 30 minutes, or maybe just 10 minutes a day, your body will feel better and, over time, get stronger and stronger. It's the same with sideways thinking. If you commit just 10 minutes a day to creative exercises you'll soon have more sideways thinking than you know what to do with. It's an inevitable output of a creative routine. An article in *Fast Company* ("How to Lead a Creative Life," December 2011) highlighted brilliant creative minds like film director Martin Scorsese. These people engage in creative exercises intuitively as part of their day-to-day routine. That is part of what makes them so creative. This book will give you tools so you can do the same.

  Stop working so hard! The answer is always more simple than the challenge!

 **Myth #4: Creativity is a point-in-time exercise.**

Quite the opposite. Creativity is an ongoing state of mind. I like to call it creative kaizen.

  Practice Creative "Kaizen": in Japanese Kai = continuous, Zen = improvement. Always wrking 2 imprv my creative mind

Creativity is part of who you are and how you act. Over time you evolve and sharpen those skills. Saying that creativity is a point-in-time exercise implies that you only whip it out for creative tasks like brainstorming, painting, or arts and crafts. Interestingly, some of the best creative problem solving happens during the least creative tasks. Never underestimate the power of sideways thinking when working on an everyday challenge or big dilemma.

Myth #5: Ah-ha's are these magical moments that randomly come to you.

Not exactly. Ah-ha moments are just the tip of the iceberg. They are the culmination of engaging in sideways exercises daily. Ah-ha moments feel magical because they're a mashup of experiences, knowledge, and data. Because it's not linear we can't always explain it, which makes it mysterious. If you want more Ah-ha moments, all you have to do is engage in more sideways activities (jump to Build It). You'll see Ah-ha tips of icebergs at every turn.

 **Myth #6: People fight innovation because they fear change.**

This is an interesting one. In Chip and Dan Heath's book *Switch: How to Change Things When Change is Hard* (Crown Business, 2010), they talk about the fact that if you take a step back and look at the human relationship to change, we actually voluntarily sign up for change all the time. We have children, we move, we switch brands, we take new jobs. So if we actually don't fear change, why do we resist innovation?

As someone wise once said, *"It's not that I don't like change, it's that I don't want to be changed."*

Nobody likes someone else telling them what to do or how to act. Think about yourself for a moment. Do you want someone else, even me, to come and tell you how to be creative? Or would you rather find and harness your own creative strengths? I call them hot spots—tiny little things that you already do that are innovative. If we can discover and harness your innovative strengths, then there is nothing to fight, because it's all bubbling up from within you. That's why this playbook has a wide range of mindsets, tools, exercises, and ideas for you. Chances are a few of them speak to your strengths, and you can use them as a springboard for unleashing even more sideways thinking.

Random idea #43598 – Small strips on sole of ur running shoes - tell u when u no longer have support. like old battery strips - green is good to go, yellow = time to change soon, red is NEED NEW SHOES BEFORE YOUR KNEES CRACK!

Myth #7: The best ideas are totally new-to-the-world, blue-sky innovations.

Not always. Take a look around your office or home. Some of the best innovations are tweaks on what already exists. The iPod was a tweak on the early, difficult-to-use digital music players. Remember those? You don't always need to comb the world for what's not yet been done. Sure, it's nice to find those things, but of equal importance are those tiny shifts. Taking something you use every day and tweaking it just 2% can make a world of difference. Tweaking led to the bendy straw, bar soap, and cup holders in cars. Take comfort in the fact that your big idea could come from a tiny but innovative tweak, or a new-to-the-world idea.

Myth #8: Imagination is purely for playtime.

So not true! It is your ultimate superpower, and to only bring it out during moments of play is a shame. You are doing yourself a huge disservice. The imagination is what allows you to create things that have not yet been created. It helps you fill the gaps and create meaning out of seemingly disparate dots of knowledge.

  Imagination def. –"forming mental images or concepts of what is not actually present to the senses; the ability to face and resolve difficulties; resourcefulness"

The Lincoln Center Institute in New York recently launched Imagination Conversations, a two-year initiative where people across the United States joined in panel discussions on how "imagination, creativity, and innovation work across sectors, and how they can be cultivated in schools and communities." The panelists, who ranged from successful entrepreneurs to academics, discussed the critical role imagination has in today's society and in their success. That's how critical imagination is beyond the playground.

a game-changing playbook for disruptive thinking

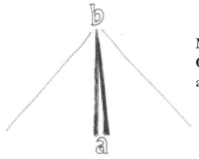

Myth #9: Imagination, Creativity, and Innovation are part of a linear process.

Not even close!

Imagination > Creativity > Innovation

These words get used interchangeably and often incorrectly. Many speak about it as a linear process. They'll say it starts with imagination, which unleashes creativity, and then the final product is innovation. In business in particular, most hold to this idea because it's easier to wrap up each step in the process with a pretty bow. In doing so we change something that should be fluid into something that's unnaturally linear. This type of thinking hinders the process because it rejects, and therefore blocks, the flexibility inherent in sideways thinking. According to Merriam-websters.com, here are the definitions for each of the elements.

Imagination: [the act or power of forming a mental image of some thing not present to the senses or never before wholly perceived in reality; ability to confront and deal with a problem]

Creativity: [ability or power to create]

Innovation: [the introduction of something new; a new idea, method, or device]

Think Sideways

You see how it might be easier to place them in a particular order. However, if you pay attention to how they operate in reality, you'll discover something very different.

In action I see it as more of a virtual and intertwined cycle. But, to be honest, I don't care which word you use as long as you're thinking sideways.

Each feeds the other. The more you engage your imagination, the more creative you are. The more creative you are, the more your imagination runs in high gear. The more you work on innovation, the more imaginative you become. Eventually they become inseparable because everything is working and the cycle is spinning so fast.

a game-changing playbook for disruptive thinking

When the cycle is spinning fast, the output is Sideways Thinking, the most powerful tool you own. Thinking Sideways helps you have a big, boisterous voice in the world.

Think Sideways

Small Insights
Make Big Differences

In 1904, the *London Daily Mirror* publicly challenged Harry Houdini to escape from a set of handcuffs that they claimed took master locksmith Nathaniel Hart several years to perfect. On the afternoon of March 17, crowds flocked to the London Hippodrome Theater in anticipation of whether Houdini would show up and accept the challenge. Much to the delight of the more than 4,000 spectators and 100 journalists, Houdini stepped onto the stage. Frank Parks, the newspaper's representative, quickly rushed over and slapped the handcuffs on Houdini. Houdini leaned in and asked if Parks wouldn't mind removing the handcuffs for a moment so that he could take off his jacket before performing. Parks was so afraid that Houdini would gather some type of insight into the workings of the handcuffs that he refused. Houdini had to use a pocketknife to cut off his jacket instead.

Then Houdini walked across the stage and behind the curtain. Fifty minutes later he emerged, handcuffs still on. His wife Bess walked across the stage, gave Houdini an encouraging kiss, and walked off. Houdini went back behind the screen. Ten minutes later he emerged, handcuff-free. The crowd went wild.

Public challenges started popping up across the globe, each claiming they had a contraption from which Houdini couldn't possibly escape.

a game-changing playbook for disruptive thinking

But there was something the public didn't know. Harry Houdini and his challengers were working together.

Houdini understood something that his competition didn't. He understood that the anticipation of the escape was as important as the escape itself. Both were part of the big act.

While his competition was following the same path, doing all the same acts, and putting up posters saying all the same things, Houdini thought sideways.

And that is why Houdini went on to become the highest-paid vaudeville act of his time, and one of the most recognized entertainers in history. Houdini was a sideways thinker.

That's also why thinking sideways has been, and always will be, the key to your competitive advantage. Sideways thinking is what separates you from the pack. Whether you are a serial entrepreneur, lifetime employee, experienced CEO, or aspiring small business owner, thinking sideways is what helps you rise above the clutter and realize your dreams— just like Houdini did in the 1900s. If Houdini was born this century, I have no doubt he would have achieved similar accomplishments with the tools available today.

a game-changing playbook for disruptive thinking

Hello, my name is Ann Tigravite...

I'm a super hero and I have the ability to defy gravity. I am impervious to negativity and naysayers. I just rise above it all. I can help others rise above the bulls*&! too if they let me. My impenetrable creative armor gives me the visionary edge I need to think big and push new ideas forward. I just float around like anything is possible. If you work with me you'll discover that you too can think big and make big things happen regardless of what others say and do.

a game-changing playbook for disruptive thinking

Hello, my name is Lye Fesucker...

I'm a super villain and with every negative word, I suck the life out of every person and every situation I encounter. I turn people into working zombies. All around me, people just agree, because they can't get a word in, and everything they say is overtaken by my negativity. Eventually everyone around me succumbs to my dreary ways. You'd better watch out because no matter how good the idea, I'm going to rain on your parade.

a game-changing playbook for disruptive thinking

SIDEWAYS
ATTITUDE
& ACTION

www.imaginibbles.com/think-sideways-playbook/

Wear these descriptors like a badge of honor!

Maverick   Rebel

Entrepreneur
          Disruptor   Believer
                    Energetic
                              Outcast
Igniter   Impatient
                    Ideator
          Creative   Creator
                    Independent
                              Outsider
                                        Unconventional
                                   Trendsetter
                    Leader
                              Original
          Resourceful

Intuitive   Imaginator
                    Eccentric   Dreamer

Rule Breaker   Visionary
                    Revolutionary   Trailblazer
          Inventive
                         Innovator

Think Sideways

I strongly believe that a big part of thinking sideways is unleashing your inner entrepreneur. The entrepreneur wants to be that maverick that pokes the bear. Great entrepreneurs intuitively think sideways. I don't mean you have to quit whatever you are doing and start a business. In fact, quit the opposite. Being an entrepreneur or disruptive thinker is more of a way of life than a job title.

That's why the first set of tools is for your attitude. They are guidelines for acting sideways all day, every day. Get into the right mindset and the actions will follow intuitively.

  Being a sideways thinker is a mindset, not a job description

Always remember that it's not about a job title. Over time I've met many sideways thinkers. Some are small business owners like Semion, who owns Semion Barbershop (a barbershop that bucked the need to be cool for a place that is welcoming and warm for all), or Gever Tulley (founder of the Brightworks alternative school in San Francisco that follows a more holistic learning approach instead of the traditional structure). Then there are those I've never met, but who we can all agree are brilliant entrepreneurs—Steve Jobs of Apple (transformed technology by making it less about the electronics and more about the human experience), J.K. Rowling, author of *Harry Potter* (went from a struggling single mother to the well-known creator of the wildly imaginative series), and Louis C.K. the comedian (willing to go against the media protocols and experiment with online sales of his work directly to fans). You'll read even more about some of these sideways thinkers and many more throughout this playbook.

a game-changing playbook for disruptive thinking

That is their gift. They are sideways thinkers.

That is what this segment is all about—getting into the sideways mindset.

Someone once asked me how I do it. How I continually have new ideas, why I chose a more entrepreneurial life instead of a more secure one, and how I often see the world differently. Most important, they asked me how I'm able to stretch beyond the obvious limits to continually disrupt the norm. That got me thinking. I've been acting this way for so long I forgot that it wasn't intuitive for everyone. As I started to crystallize the sideways thinking mindset for myself, I started to wonder deeply about other entrepreneurs. So I did what any curious bird would do, and I started studying them (jump to Stalking). I searched out every interview, commencement speech, article, and blog I could find, looking for the thread that tied them all together. When it all started coming together I jumped up and did the chicken dance. Not because what they did was so surprising or unique. No, because the behaviors they exhibited were things that anyone could do with a little coaching. How cool is that? Anyone can be a sideways thinker.

What they don't have in common is their job title. They come from different backgrounds, are armed with different dreams, and took wildly different paths in life. But if you take a step back and study them, you'll see that what they have in common is a mindset. It's that mindset that allows them to see things so differently, to make art out of trash and blaze new trails, leaving big footprints as they go.

They come from all walks of life like you and me, but their mindset is what sets them apart and sets them up for greatness.

a game-changing playbook for disruptive thinking

Get your greatness hat on, because if you change how you think inside, then the outside actions and results will come naturally. You may have doubts. You may wonder if you are a sideways thinker or not. If any or all of these statements apply to you then yes, you have it in you:

- Your rebellious side gets incredibly frustrated by a play-it-safe culture.

- Your inner entrepreneur keeps nudging you to break the rules.

- Something deep down feels the need to disrupt the status quo.

- You desperately want to get out of that box you are trapped in.

- The words on the cover of this book—sideways, disruptive, game-changing—spoke to you.

- Your right brain feels exhausted and needs a push to get energized.

It's not about if you are pursuing that big idea or just getting through the day. It's about what you want to do and how you want to be. Perhaps you're already out there shaking it up and want to build on your momentum. Perhaps you just need to get unstuck because, no matter how hard you try to suppress it, something inside you keeps screaming for more. I believe this with every bone in my body. We all have it in us some way or another. It's just a matter of mobilizing our inner sideways and letting it out into the world.

As you delve into this segment, take some time to examine how you behave every day. You may find you are missing some of these and need to dial up others. These are exercises and tools to get your attitude in the right place for sideways thinking.

Write a Manifesto

This is your foundation. A manifesto is a set of beliefs you hold so deeply that they can't help but guide you. Your manifesto informs the decisions you make, the actions you take, and the trails you blaze.

Find something you believe in so strongly that it physically pulls you in that direction. A manifesto is a way of life. Great entrepreneurs and sideways thinkers use their manifesto to drive the businesses they lead.

Sideways Thinkers who have a vivid manifesto also have an unavoidable gravitational pull. People can't help but be drawn to them. People want to be around them, to be a part of their disruptive dreams.

Part of this gravitational pull comes from the confidence they ooze in who they are and what they're trying to do in this world. It also emanates from their natural ability to communicate their manifesto through every word and action.

This is my copy of my manifesto:

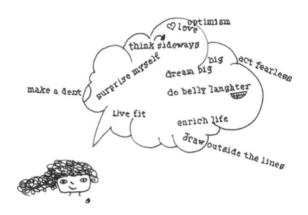

Think Sideways

My manifesto ultimately guided me to create imaginibbles, an edu-tainment company dedicated to spreading innovation like wildfire. If you click on the "About" page on our website (www.imaginibbles.com/about) you'll find:

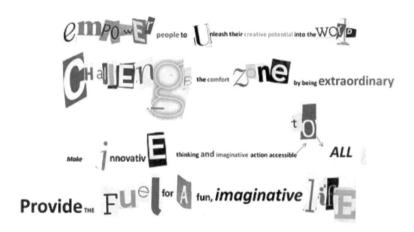

This is a set of beliefs that has guided many of my actions. Those who see it know exactly what we believe in and what we're trying to do in the world. The company is a direct expression of my personal manifesto.

Have you ever shopped at Lululemon? Lululemon is a line of yoga-inspired ath-leisure wear. If you do shop there you get a bag for your purchases that looks like this:

a game-changing playbook for disruptive thinking

That's their manifesto on the bag—a set of beliefs that guides them, and in turn guides their customers. When Chip Wilson founded Lululemon he didn't create a typical mission and vision statement. Instead, if you went to their website you found their manifesto. You can feel and see their beliefs in everything they do—the goal tracker online and the yoga lovers who work in their stores. Their manifesto inspires them and their customers. Lululemon lovers proudly reuse their bags to carry everything from groceries to gym clothes. They're telling the world that they too believe in living the Lululemon life. That's all because Chip Wilson believes deeply that everyone should rise above mediocrity and live a life of greatness.

  Random idea #10009 a mat made out of sticky yoga mat material you put under your wheels to keep you from getting stuck in the snow. Slip under front of wheels and ride out of parking spot (or ditch)

Think Sideways

That's their manifesto on the bag—a set of beliefs that guides them, and in turn guides their customers. When Chip Wilson founded Lululemon he didn't create a typical mission and vision statement. Instead, if you went to their website you found their manifesto. You can feel and see their beliefs in everything they do—the goal tracker online and the yoga lovers who work in their stores. Their manifesto inspires them and their customers. Lululemon lovers proudly reuse their bags to carry everything from groceries to gym clothes. They're telling the world that they too believe in living the Lululemon life. That's all because Chip Wilson believes deeply that everyone should rise above mediocrity and live a life of greatness.

  Random idea #10009 a mat made out of sticky yoga mat material you put under your wheels to keep you from getting stuck in the snow. Slip under front of wheels and ride out of parking spot (or ditch)

Think Sideways

When the mind zeros in on a manifesto with belief and clarity, everything is possible. Your entire mental and physical state changes. It's crazy to see what happens to people when they have something to believe in.

I'm sure you are seeing the trend here. Manifestos are as important to you, the individual, as they are to those around you. Manifestos, when crystal clear, are so powerful that people can't help but jump onboard.

If you know what your manifesto is but it's locked up inside your head, then bring it to life visually. A daily reminder of your manifesto can inspire you when you are feeling down, get you unstuck when your wheels are in the mud, and make a difficult decision seem crystal clear.

If you don't yet have that driving force, don't worry—you aren't alone. The hardest part can be figuring out what drives you. I equate it to finding the right wall for your ladder.

There I was at the top of the corporate ladder looking around. I was in my best business suit. I had these fitted, black Ann Taylor suit pants with a matching waist-length jacket and, of course, I was wearing a red button-down business shirt because at some point someone had told me that red was the power color for women. My hair was pulled back in a low pony to make sure everyone knew I meant business.

Yup, there I was…

But the view at the top was not what I expected, and the more I looked around, the more I felt anger and frustration instead of the feelings I was supposed to have, like confidence and joy. The suit I was wearing started to not feel right, and I didn't feel comfortable in my own skin.

The one good thing about all these feelings rising to the top was that they forced me to pause.

To pause, take a moment, and actually look down and around the ladder. Something I hadn't done before.

See, I jumped on the ladder in 1995 after graduating from the University of California Berkeley. I quickly climbed up the ladder one rung at a time. Sometimes I would jump off and do my own entrepreneurial things, some wildly successful, some wild failures. It was probably my first clue that the corporate ladder was the wrong place for me, but I would keep jumping back on and climbing up. Along the way I worked with giants of industry like General Mills, Clorox, IBM, and Procter & Gamble. In fact, some of the products I created are on supermarket shelves today. I was proud of those accomplishments and kept on going up that ladder. Suddenly there I was, standing at the top at age 35 being groomed to take over a multi-million dollar brand strategy and innovation consultancy.

But when I finally took a moment to look down at the rungs on the ladder, I realized something very painful. With every rung I climbed up, my desire to be edgy and take risks had gone down. I started to stuff my imaginative ways, my more innovative ideas into the drawer until eventually that part of me suffocated.

The entrepreneurial spirit that I, and all of us, was born with had vanished as I tried to follow in OTHERS' footsteps, as I tried to be professional, to be what I thought was expected of me and of business.

Soaking in the full view for the first time in a long time, I realized something...

My ladder was on the wrong wall! I had forgotten my personal manifesto!

I grabbed my things, got into my best Heisman pose, and ran for it.

I created my own wall and painted my manifesto all over it. I've been climbing the ladder on the imaginibbles wall ever since. I'm not sure if I'm at the top or not, but I know I'm loving every rung on my ladder.

  Climbing up? Make sure ur ladder is even on the right wall!

It's very fulfilling to have something to believe in, and more importantly, it gives you the confidence to take those bold leaps and to challenge the rules because you know it's the right thing to do. It's your manifesto. And yes, throughout history manifestos have been used for evil, nefarious purposes (insert stereotypically evil laugh). Let's agree that for our purposes we'll use it do what makes us happy and to fulfill our big dreams.

You didn't think we'd stop here did you?

Here is the worksheet for creating your manifesto. If you would like the full-page version of this exercise, follow the QR Code.

www.imaginibbles.com/think-sideways-playbook/

Manifesto Worksheet

Step one: Draw how you look and feel when you are at your best. Think about how you act, what you are doing, what you might be saying, and how you interact with the world.

Step two: Complete these statements (you may have one or multiple
answers to each. If you think it, write it down.

I want to be _bold, happy, edgy, fun, successful_

I want to have _freedom (time), $$ security, connection to world_

I want to create _products that help others, a business my family can be a part of_

I believe you should _learn something new_ daily

I want to change _balance in my life - MORE!_

I want to accomplish _everything → successful new venture_

I want to be known for _being one gets it done where other fail_

Twelve months from now I want to say that I _launched my idea, added 8hrs more free time to week, drum up in motion_

My biggest dreams include _being on morning news, going to Africa, experiencing something amazing_

Step three: With a colorful pen go back and circle up to ten of your
words or phrases.

imaginibbles
...think sideways

a game-changing playbook for disruptive thinking

Step four: Create your manifesto by transforming the words you circled into a colorful flag. Fill the flag up completely with your manifesto—words, pictures, a combo of both. Express yourself in a way that works for you.

Step five: Post your Manifesto Flag somewhere visible.

Think Sideways

I also suggest you take your manifesto and make it wallet-size. All you have to do is take your visual collage or piece of paper to a copy center and ask them to shrink and laminate. It's a nice reminder of what you are working towards.

PS—Speaking of copying, did you know that Kinko's was founded by Paul "Kinko" Orfalea, who rented a space next to a hamburger stand near the University of California Santa Barbara campus for $100 a month to sell pens, notebooks, and copy services after he realized that the school library only had one copy machine for thousands of students? He thought that this new technology was amazing and should be offered to more than just a few, so with 2.5-cent copies he built a business. Another true Sideways Thinker.

Eternal Optimism

Sideways thinkers are eternal optimists. I'm not saying they are always in a good mood or walk around with a weird perma-grin, but, deep down, Sideways Thinkers believe that there's always another opportunity waiting around the corner. We all know about the great innovator Walt Disney. But did you know that Mickey Mouse as we know him today was not the first character he created to drive his dreams? It was his second. His first design was stolen from him and therefore not usable. So while sitting on a train he sketched a new character. This one was a mouse with big ears and big feet. I'm sure Walt Disney was angry, but his actions showed that he was an eternal optimist. Some of us would have thrown in the towel or wallowed in the fact that our big idea was taken from us, but not Walt Disney. A setback, even a big one, wasn't going to hold him back. I suppose you have to be an optimist to envision an amusement park in the middle of the desert in southern California.

It's hard to imagine given the park's greatness and the company's impact that at one time a man with a vision stood in the middle of an empty dust bowl of a desert and envisioned a land full of magic.

Every entrepreneur I've ever spoken to has talked about the need to stay positive. In the face of so many "no's," and you'll get a lot of them, you have to believe that a "yes" is right around the corner (jump to Depart from the Text). That positivity keeps them from throwing in the towel when things get tough. It keeps them searching for another solution when setbacks throw them off, and it gives them the ability to find opportunity in the toughest obstacles.

Sometimes optimism is hard to maintain, and I'm not saying that every day will be sunny and perfect. But being optimistic reminds you that rainy days do end, and that even rainy days can teach you something.

There isn't a switch that you can flip to suddenly become optimistic. I wish there were. I like to go back to the old phrase, "Fake it till you make it." If you tell yourself enough times that you're an optimist, eventually you will feel it in your core. When you are out there in the world, remind yourself that one, two, even twenty big ideas are all around you; that every setback is simply an opportunity to come up with a new solution.

It's no surprise that optimism leads to perseverance, and if you are going to be a sideways thinker, then you have to recognize that it takes a lot of perseverance. Being entrepreneurial is a lifelong journey. Whether it's working to shift a company culture or open up the shop you've always dreamed of, it takes perseverance to see it through.

Nothing happens ovenight. In his book *Outliers: The Story of Success* (Little, Brown and Company, 2008), Malcolm Gladwell talks about the fact that it takes 10,000 hours of practice to become an expert at something. That's a lot of practice!

Nothing gets u 2 overnight success faster than a few years of hard work and lots of caffeine

I was listening to the radio in my rental car during a trip back east for an innovation workshop when I found a Beatles music marathon punctuated by interviews with Paul McCartney. The radio host asked McCartney what it felt like when they landed their first big record deal, and if they felt this intense pressure to be creative and come up with new songs. McCartney said something very interesting. He said that by the time they got into their first recording session, they could have recorded eight hours worth of songs. The Beatles had played together for a long time before they were discovered. They persevered through late-night shows, unpaid gig after gig, and many nearly-empty venues before they became pop sensations.

It takes optimism and perseverance.

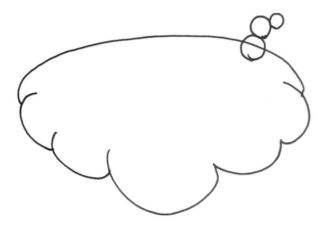

a game-changing playbook for disruptive thinking

Keep Your Antennas Up

It's my husband's 40th birthday, so I take him out to a downtown dive bar. We are hanging out, enjoying a few drinks, when the door blows open. At first I turn away as I'm hit by a blast of cold air. I turn back to watch a pack of revelers all dressed in Snuggies® with hats and belts and jewelry piling into the bar. I'm so shocked by their appearance that I have to ask what's going on. I turn to the leader of the pack and ask, "What are you guys doing?" In the way only a drunk twenty-something could respond, she yells, "It's a Snuggie® bar crawl, Woooooooo!!!"

In response I gave the leader of the Snuggie® pack a very perplexing look, and she went on to say that Snuggie® bar crawls are popular across the country and that most of her friends have done it.

What?! This campy infomercial that I saw at two in the morning during a bad bout of insomnia has gone from a cheesy TV spot to something hip and cool with Generation Y? That didn't compute for me, not even after a few drinks. It's a blanket with holes in it! In my house, blankets with holes in them are not called "Snuggies®." They're called "rags."

Did you know that as of 2010, this blanket with holes in it has sold more than 20 million units? I'm sure you've watched the infomercial or seen a Snuggie® at a major retailer. I'm guessing you might even be wearing one right now, but are too embarrassed to ever admit it.

I'm sure you've had one of those moments, like I had at the bar, where you see something like the Snuggie® bar crawl that makes you go, "What??!!" Normally you just shrug and move on.

Whatever it is, it probably isn't important enough to pay attention to, and without a doubt, it has no relevance to your life.

What if, next time, you stopped and paid attention! What I saw that night wasn't a random, who-cares thing. What I caught was a glimpse of someone who thought sideways, doing something unconventional and charting new territory. In the case of the Snuggie®, that's more than $200 million dollars worth.

There is a lot of sideways thinking going on out there, but you have to keep your antennas up and your mind open. Those glimpses of someone else's sideways thinking will help you think sideways. You'll begin to see things in a new light. You'll connect the random dots (jump to Go Wide) and start ideas percolating.

Great sideways thinkers always have their antennas up. It's part of how they walk through the world. When those antennas are up they spot everything, especially the more innovative things. You'll make connections between seemingly unrelated events, and you'll use those connections to create new ideas. You'll take note of how someone else is doing things and learn from their best practices. You'll get those juices flowing sideways purely by being immersed in the world around you. You'll spot opportunities where others see blank space. To do all that, you gotta get those antennas up.

To sharpen this part of your mind when you're at your desk, subscribe to newsletters like Springwise.com. They have spotters who scour the globe for cool and innovative ideas. Subscribe to Groupon.com. I know the deals are tempting, but what I've found even more interesting is the occasional super-cool idea that I would have never known about otherwise.

Kelly, who works at the imaginarium, has a funny little quirk. She wears gloves when she drinks a bottle of beer. She wants to keep her hands warm, and that's not easy to do with an ice-cold beer in her hands. While writing this book, I took a break to check out the daily deals from Groupon.com and there it was—the Sküüzi, a Scandinavian-designed, mitten-esque beverage holder handmade from cozy Merino wool. No joke, this exists! Just like the Snuggie®, I think it's strangely innovative. Instead of brushing over the need to keep your hands warm and your beer cold, someone actually turned that insight into this fantastic product. You know you want one!

We have a policy at imaginibbles. If you see something innovative, you must either take a picture of it or buy it and bring it in for show-and-tell. I have windowsills piled with the latest discoveries. They keep my antennas up, and on a down day, they provide me with much-needed inspiration. You never know where one of those finds will take you.

Think Sideways

Again, keeping the antennas up means you start to pay attention to the stuff that's going on near the fringes. You'll start to see trends before they go mainstream.

Keeping your antennas up not only means that you start to notice innovative things happening all around you, it also means that you'll start to see ideas and opportunities for your life and work.

This guy walked by me with a super-cool T-shirt. It was black with a large skull and crossbones on the front, only the skull part wasn't a skull, it was a cupcake. Two days later, I'm in my favorite cupcake shop and I see this logo again on a postcard at the counter. My antennas are up now and I'm getting curious. What is this cupcake thing I keep seeing? The postcard says "Johnny Cupcakes," so I go online to Johnnycupcakes.com and check it out. Now my antennas are tingling. I had come across a totally innovative person and business. Johnny Cupcakes is a lifestyle brand with some of the most loyal followers I have ever seen. His website is basic, but dynamic. His T-shirts are funky and irreverent, and his videos give a glimpse of a guy and a brand that are shaking it up.

The light bulb goes off. In the back of my mind, a challenge was brewing.

How do I make this concept of spreading innovation like wildfire happen?
How do I make innovation accessible to all?

a game-changing playbook for disruptive thinking

Many in my own circle told me that I had to have a book. They would say, "Without a book you can't be an author, and therefore, an authority." That advice just didn't sit right with me, but until I saw Johnny Cupcakes, I didn't know what to do with it. Checking out this apparel company gave me an idea. Instead of a complicated creativity book or game or toy, I would create T-shirts. Each shirt would have a visual representation of living an innovative life. One might tell you to Veer Off, another to Innovate. After all, what's more accessible and universal than a T-shirt? With my antennas up, I solved a problem and launched a successful product line. If I hadn't noticed the guy walking down the street or the postcards on the counter, I may not have connected the dots and created products imaginators across the globe love.

Think Sideways

Sideways Thinkers are always keeping their antennas up. Never pass up an opportunity to explore.

When you get the, "What's going on here?" feeling, stop and pay attention.

When you see something that catches your eye, ask, "Why?" When you encounter something that makes you tilt your head and go, "What??!!" learn more.

Don't let a moment go by where your nostrils aren't picking up the scent of sideways thinking. Carry around this worksheet and jot down everything your antennas pick up. Follow the QR Code to download.

And yes, I am a proud owner of a Snuggie®.

www.imaginibbles.com/think-sideways-playbook/

a game-changing playbook for disruptive thinking

Antennas Up Worksheet

Keep track of all things that caught your attention and why. Don't forget to ask yourself:

Why is....interesting to me?

What can I learn from.... ?

What can....teach me ?

Now that I know about...what should I do about it?

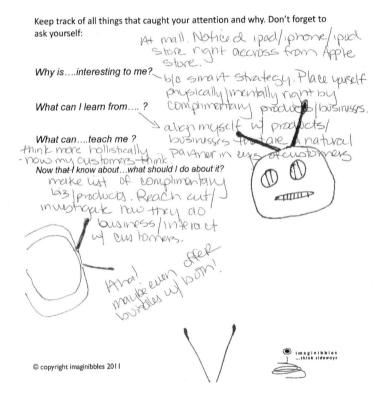

At mall. Notice d ipad/iphone/ipod store right accross from Apple store.

b/c smart strategy. Place yourself physically/mentally right by complimentary products/businesses.

→ align myself w/ products/ businesses that are a natural partner in eyes of customers

think more hollistically - how my customers think

make list of complimentary products. Reach out/ investigate how they do business/interact w/ customers.

Aha! maybe even offer bundles w/ both!

imaginibbles
...think sideways

Think Sideways

Jump on Two

We were rattling along the road through dense Costa Rican jungle in a ratty, rented Jeep when my good friend and travel partner yelled out. I couldn't quite understand her over the rattle and rumble of the makeshift plastic windows, but I saw the hand-lettered sign propped up against the rock.

"Bungee Jumping Next Right."

We veered off the main road and followed a series of cardboard arrows directing us this way and that, until we came upon a rusty, abandoned bridge spanning a very, very deep ravine. We pulled up just as another pair of tourists was getting out of their car, clearly craving some off-the-beaten-path adventure.

The four of us, all outfitted in matching lightweight REI travel clothes, signed in at the weathered shack and made our way to the center of the bridge.

A nice young man with a big pearly-white smile and a heap of gear at his feet greeted us on the bridge. In his best English he said, "Who wants to go first?"

We stood there, tongue-tied, looking alternately over the railing, then at each other, then down into the ravine. At the bottom was a sparkling trickle of water winding between ginormous boulders. Bravely, the other pair of travelers offered to go first. I didn't argue.

One by one I watched them make the leap from the bridge, petrified, and then come bouncing back up with a look of sheer joy on their faces.

a game-changing playbook for disruptive thinking

Then it was my turn. I don't remember getting rigged up, or the nice young man putting the straps around my ankles, or him attaching those straps to a rope that eventually was attached to the bridge.

I was numb with fear. I snapped out of it just as I was being hoisted up onto the railing.

I stood there with nothing to hold, my legs shaking violently, and my heart pounding so hard I could see it through my shirt. I heard the nice young man say, "I'm going to count to three. On three you are going to jump up and away from the bridge."

"I can remember that," I thought, "Go on 3, go on 3…" And he started counting…1……….2……….
…And I jumped.

I couldn't wait. Somehow I knew that if I waited one more second, I would lose my nerve and jump back down onto the safety of the bridge.

But when my feet left the railing and I was soaring through the air, I went from living in fear to living in freedom. I had never felt anything so liberating, so ex-hilarating.

As I was being hoisted back up I promised myself that I would never forget that one second. And I've never regretted the decision to follow that cardboard sign through the jungle to jump off an abandoned bridge. Being bold enough to stand out in the sea of sameness is a lot like bungee jumping. One second can make the difference between taking the leap to new heights or turning around to face the same old things you've always done.

As people, entrepreneurs, and business executives, we often wait just one second too long, and in that one second we talk ourselves out of doing the very things that we most want to do; things that seem risky or challenging. We narrow, instead of widen, our focus, and therefore miss the great flashes of innovation staring us in the face.

Great sideways thinkers have learned to summon the courage to jump on two. Ask yourself, when was the last time you jumped on two and pursued that great Ah-ha? When did you allow one more second to get in the way of taking that leap?

You may call it thinking things through. I call it waiting one second too long. Don't let analysis paralysis stop you. Don't let that inner voice that over-thinks everything get in your way.

It only takes one second for a great idea to be brushed aside. It only takes one second for a brilliant dream to die.

Jump on two.

Don't Step Outside Your Comfort Zone

I've never understood why people try to get others to step outside their comfort zone. Why would anyone want to do that? It's scary and all you really want to do is jump back into the warm safety of your comfort zone. When you ask people to step outside of their comfort zone, you are reinforcing the fact that they'll never get comfortable doing it, and while you are out there in scary zone, you'd much rather be back in your comfy zone.

Some of you may seem a little surprised with what you just read given my love of taking risks and trying new things. But I don't see anything I do as stepping outside my comfort zone. Instead, I think of it as expanding my comfort zone. Everything I do that initially makes my heart race and my legs go numb is just another addition to my ever-expanding comfort zone. That simple shift in mindset puts me at ease and increases my willingness to do things that scare me. That's because I know that after I do them once, they'll never scare me again. When I launched my first entrepreneurial venture, Stayingfit.com (you've never heard of it because it bombed), I was petrified. But knowing that I'd never be that scared again bolstered my willingness to take the leap. Now, five businesses later, including a fitness business that turned into studios in multiple states, a nationally-published book, *Bootcamp360 for Brides* by Harper Collins, and several discussions with movie and TV production houses, I don't fear that first step.

Turn your thoughts into Hollywood storyboards. With a blank piece of paper, create twelve frames with lines underneath. Draw your thoughts and add captions. Let your story organically come to life from one frame to the next.

imaginibbles.com

Find a quote about imagination that speaks to you. Write it on a sticky note and place it somewhere visible. Look at it frequently during the day.

imaginibbles.com

Quick, don't think, just ask. Grab one of your old Q&A games and without hesitation answer the questions. They key is to not spend a lot of time pondering the answer – just go for it.

imaginibbles.com

Think back to when you were a child. What was your favorite thing to do – skipping, crab walk, hopscotch, jumping rope? Find the movement that makes you smile and do it for five minutes.

imaginibbles.com

a game-changing playbook for disruptive thinking

Obsess

Obsession counts more than anything!

Emma is the owner of The Shoppe, a cupcake and cereal café in Denver. Cupcakes are all the rage, but her place isn't like all the others. I asked her why she would open a cupcake shop at the peak of the trend. I think there are literally cupcakes shops on every corner. She replied that she hadn't opened a cupcake shop. She opened a place where she could engage in her obsession for baking and create a place where everyone can be a kid. Her shop has funky art on the walls, board games for families to share, hip-hop music in the background, and anime on the massive wall-mounted TV. Her cupcakes have names like "Death by Chocolate" and "Pineapple Express." Her "Snickerdoodle" cupcake literally tastes like the cookie it's named for. I swear, the "Banana Split" is better than the real thing. Now that your mouth is watering and you are scouring the pantry for chocolate, let's talk about Emma. Emma isn't your traditional cupcake shop owner. She never went to baking school. She didn't get an MBA or take courses in finance. Simply put, Emma has an obsession and a deep love for creating her dream.

Skills are easy to come by. Obsession is hard. As they say, do what you love and love what you do. Her place is funky, fun, and totally unique. It wasn't experience that drove her to open one of the most successful shops in Denver. It was her obsession. If you obsess, you can figure out the skills and experience to get it done.

Finding your obsession can come from a lot of places. It can come from looking at your strengths, your experiences, and your loves. Take some time to crystallize your passions, because somewhere in there is an obsession that will turn into your next big idea.

Random idea #349358 – parking meters that automatically give you an extra 15 mins after time is up. Put in cc card, get your 2 hours. If late, meter charges you an extra 25 cents. It knows your car and when you leave.

If you are at the stage where you are still searching for your passion, don't worry. It's there; you just don't see it yet. I created the exercises below just for you. A woman emailed me about one of my keynote speeches she had attended. She felt moved and wanted to explore her passions, so I sent her some worksheets I had created for a training session on this exact topic.

She then got a few friends together and had an imaginibbles day in the park where they worked together to figure out their passions and ideate where that could take them.

You can do these sheets solo or grab a picnic lunch and head out to the park with a few friends. The exercise is 5 pages of worksheets, so follow the QR Code to download them.

www.imaginibbles.com/think-sideways-playbook/

a game-changing playbook for disruptive thinking

76

Follow Frustration

Have you ever felt so frustrated by something you felt compelled to fix it?

When Elizabeth and Joan from Clouds and Stars were new moms, they were frustrated because, as any new mother can tell you, changing a crib sheet is a Herculean task. You have to take out the blankets, teddy bears, and other paraphernalia. Then you have to remove the crib bumper. Next, you have to contort your body as you lean into the crib, balance on the dresser, and try to lift the tight-fitting mattress and pull off the sheet. Babies make messes daily, so sheet changing is part of the routine. That frustration led to an idea, and the QuickZip sheet was born. QuickZip is exactly what it sounds like. You literally zip off the top part of the sheet. No more body contortions.

It's easy to get frustrated, but opportunity lurks behind frustration. Keep these worksheets with you and every time you get that "grrrrr" feeling, whip them out and spend a moment following your frustration.

Think Sideways

Keep track of "if only" moments

I wish there was a product that made me get up + go to the gym!

Why can't this product be easy + affordable

I want a better way to get up in the morning

I wouldn't be so frustrated if my alarm wasn't loud, annoying, and jolting.

I need something that is soothing yet gets me excited to get out of my warm, comfy bed.

Ideas: blinds that open on a timer so the sun is your alarm,
a yoga class that shows up at your door (rather you going to it), an
accountability team that keeps all team members on track
by having a telephone chain wake up call, yoga clothes
you can sleep in.

imaginibbles
...think sideways

a game-changing playbook for disruptive thinking

A reminder to follow the QR Code for a download of this worksheet

www.imaginibbles.com/think-sideways-playbook/

  Random idea #43059458 portable sound absorbing wall dividers – perfect for any restaurant w. rude/loud ppl. Folds up – keep in purse – whip out anywhere

Believe You Can Defy the Odds

If you visit New York's Lower West Side, don't miss a walk on the High Line. The High Line is a 13-mile stretch of elevated train tracks that have been transformed into a park. During the early part of the 20th century there were so many accidents between street traffic and freight cars that 10th avenue was known as Death Avenue. At one point, the city tried putting men on horses to wave red flags in front of the train for safety. In 1929 the elevated tracks were approved, and eventually opened for freight trains in 1934. The High Line was built 30 feet above the ground in order to get the trains off of the streets.

With the rise of interstates in the 1950s, the railways became less relevant. The final freight car—three cars carrying frozen turkeys—rode across the High Line in 1980.

In 1999, the approximately one-mile stretch of track in the meatpacking district of New York City was on the verge of being demolished. Local residents Joshua David and Robert Hammond lobbied to have the structure revived and turned into open space. The neighborhood rallied in a surprising effort to save and revive this decrepit hunk of metal.

It took several years, grant proposals, and committee sessions to see their dream realized. In December of 2002 their dreams became a reality, and city policy was formed to preserve and reuse the High Line tracks.

While the neighborhood had a deep passion for reviving the dilapidated structure, they also recognized that this was an opportunity to do something innovative. It was as if they were working with a blank slate. Instead of trying to solve the challenge themselves, they created "Design the High Line," an idea competition that anyone could enter. Proposals came in from 720 teams across 36 countries. They varied from elevated housing to a mile-long swimming pool, with all kinds of ideas in between.

The winning proposal turned the High Line into a dynamic open-space park that respects its history and brings to life the synergy between the industrial and the natural.

Joshua and Robert are true sideways thinkers. The High Line story is full of sideways thinking, but I'm going to focus on a very important aspect of the sideways attitude.

Sideways thinkers believe they can defy the odds. And because they believe so strongly, they often do.

First, what are the odds that anyone wanted to do anything but tear down the imposing structure? Second, what are the odds that two neighborhood locals could push it all the way through from an idea to a City Council vote? Any finally, what are the odds that the world would take interest in a tiny slice of NYC to submit hundreds of innovative ideas? The odds were against them every step of the way, yet today when you get off the A subway at 14th Street and walk west, you'll find hundreds of people enjoying beautiful open space including grassland areas, a sundeck, and even a water feature.

  "Innovation thrives when the odds are deeply against it."

I've often wondered why innovation thrives when everything is working against it. I think it's because you have nothing to lose. It's either all or nothing, so you might as well dream big. When you are working towards incremental baby steps it's easy to fall into old patterns and accept failure. The stakes are low and the benefits minimal. The High Line's innovators teach us that having the odds against you could be the best thing that can happen. It gives you permission to leap instead of hop, run versus walk. You have all the room you want to be innovative instead of being shackled by boundaries. When your dream is so big it seems crazy, others expect nothing but innovation. You have to think a little sideways to even take on the challenge after all.

It's a blessing. Most people run from a big challenge, but sideways thinkers turn their head toward the storm and charge into a challenge.

Think Sideways

The next time someone offers you an opportunity to take on something that seems out-of-this-world, jump on it!

There Are No Rules!

There is a big misconception that the rules have changed and now we all have to scramble to figure out how to play by the new rules. It puts us into catch-up mode. I think that's totally inaccurate. It's not that the rules have changed; it's that there are no rules. While some may see the economic environment we live in as total chaos, I see it as gigantic opportunity slapping me across the face. It hurt a bit at first, but wow, after the sting subsided I realized I'm looking at a world where any and every path to success is possible. It's true for me, and it's true for you too. In my web series imagi-NATION™ we showcase disruptive innovators that are creating their own rules and their own paths to success. Look around your neighborhood. How many totally new concepts have popped up in the past three years? Once you get your antennas up I bet you'll see quite a few.

There is B-cycle, which implemented a totally new concept—a bike-sharing system that offers pay-as-you-go and membership options at bike stations across Denver—because of their desire to get more people out of cars and onto bikes. If you have a meeting across town there is no need to fight traffic. Just swipe your card, grab a bike, and go.

I wonder, did B-cycle follow the rules or create their own? I think you know the answer. There were no preexisting rules in their business, so they created their own and it worked. Thousands of Denverites and tourists now take rides on B-cycles every month.

When I decided to transform imaginibbles into an edu-tainment company that focused on everyday people and aspiring entrepreneurs, I got a lot of resistance. The traditional model for this type of business is to focus on process-driven innovation at a corporate level. I said, "No thanks." I'm more interested in effecting change at the human level. Most told me I wasn't following the rules of success, but we have so aptly proven them wrong. I can make up my own rules. And that is exactly what I've done. I could have just blended in with all the others, but I prefer to make a dent and play in new territory.

```
S
M
A
S
H
T
H                     C
E
B R E A K T H E R U L E S
  U                       E
  L                         A
  E                           T   N
  S                               E
                                  W
                                  R U L E S
```

Learn in Motion

Look to the distant horizon and wave your magic wand, sending good vibes out into the universe. Then return home and wait. Wait for the big idea, wait for the Ah-ha moment, wait for the stars to align.

As Dr. Seuss so wonderfully stated in his book *Oh, the Places You'll Go* (Random House Children's Books):

> *Waiting for the fish to bite*
> *or waiting for wind to fly a kite*
> *or waiting around for Friday night*
> *or waiting, perhaps, for their Uncle Jake*
> *or a pot to boil, or a Better Break*
> *or a string of pearls, or a pair of pants*
> *or a wig with curls, or Another Chance.*
> *Everyone is just waiting.*
>
> *NO!*
> *That's not for you!*
>
> *Somehow you'll escape*
> *all that waiting and staying.*
> *You'll find the bright places*
> *where Boom Bands are playing.*

It doesn't get better than a Dr. Seuss quote! But, on a serious note, Dr. Seuss made an important point that we can all learn. Waiting around for that great thing is a cycle that's hard to get out of, and usually it doesn't amount to much, especially when it comes to sideways endeavors.

I like to flip that old phrase "Good things come to those who wait" into "Good things come to those who DON'T WAIT." Get out there and build, learn, grow, and discover.

Someone close to me is very interested in starting his own liquor company, and hard apple cider in particular. He has a full-time job in finance, a wife, two kids, a dog, and lots of housework. At this stage, he has two options. One is to wait for all the pieces to fall into place. Maybe the job slows down (unlikely), the kids get older (too far away), and the house maintains itself (never gonna happen). Option two is to take small steps toward his big entrepreneurial dreams.

Let's face it, option one is the waiting game and option two is the action game. Instead of waiting for those good things to happen, he's making things happen in a good way. He brews his own cider after the kids go to bed. Then, if a friend pops by, he gives them a taste and asks for feedback. He even has a name and label that he mocked up on his own. He is on his way.

You can be on your way too. Stop waiting. You have to get impatient and take action.

Life is Good started by selling T-shirts out of the back of a van. I saw the founder of White Girl Salsa doing taste-testing tables at Whole Foods Market. A colleague came to my home to hold mini-focus groups with a few mom friends for a new baby product she has in mind. She showed them simple prototypes and a marketing statement and gathered a wealth of feedback before going to the second round of prototyping. They are all on their way.

There are two ends of the spectrum. At one end are people who like to wait until the path is totally mapped out and all the lights are green before they begin their journey. No surprise that they spend most of their time planning and little or none doing.

On the other side of the spectrum are those sideways thinkers who prefer to learn in motion. They get in their cars and go. Every mile is a learning mile. If the light turns red, they just turn right. If one street is blocked, they find a different route.

a game-changing playbook for disruptive thinking

Get into the habit of learning in motion. Ask yourself, "How can I get this out of my head and out into the real world?" or "How can I learn while moving forward at the same time?" The answer to those questions should get the wheels turning.

  Random idea #945834 – a sensor I can stick to the skin on my arm that tells me when I've had too much caffeine – right now it would be beeping!

Dream Crazy

Google has an innovative series where they bring in various celebrities, authors, and experts to speak at their @Google Talks. You can find many of their interviews and keynotes on Youtube.com (user: AtGoogleTalks). One in particular caught my attention. It was an interview with Lady Gaga. It was at the start of the interview when she said something that made me smile. She said, "All my high school friends wanted to get jobs here. I wanted to be what they were searching for." A simple yet profoundly insightful statement. Whether you love or hate her music, Lady Gaga has become a force in the industry. More importantly, her statement shows that before becoming a mega-star, Lady Gaga had a crazy-big dream. Don't be afraid to dream crazy-big. The bigger, the crazier, the better. Crazy-big dreams brought us amusement parks in the middle of a desert (Disneyland), musical movements (The Beatles), a revolution in school cafeterias (Ann Cooper, the Renegade Lunch Lady), apparel manufactured in the United States (American Apparel), and the invention of an entirely new category called lifestyle design (Tim Ferriss and *The 4-Hour Workweek*).

Life is too short to have mediocre
dreams. Go crazy-big or go away

Go in the Opposite Direction

Louis C.K. is a well-known comedian with multiple TV specials
and an Emmy-nominated show, *Louie*. His comedy is raw, insightful, and often centered around being a dad. Recently, Louis did
the unthinkable. He recorded his stand-up show at the Beacon
Theater in Manhattan, then posted the recording for sale on his
website for $5 a download. Instead of taking the typical path of
packing it into DVDs and selling it through a partnership with
a TV studio, he went directly to the people. Industry types said
he was crazy. They told him to do anything but that. They said it
wouldn't work, it would never make money, and that the experiment would fail. So naturally, he went for it, and sure enough it's
been a wild success. Hours after posting, more than 50,000 people
downloaded the show at five bucks a pop. (More than 110,000
people have downloaded it as of December 2011. Do the math.)

By doing the opposite of everyone's advice, Louis C.K.
set a new precedent. Now they aren't talking about whether his
experiment was crazy, but speculating about which comedians will
follow his example.

His story shows us something powerful. It shows us that
to disrupt that status quo, you have to go against the grain. You
have to take in that advice and then do the opposite.
Do exactly what they tell you not to do.

Have you ever watched the various evening news programs and wondered if they were all reading the same teleprompter? No matter which channel you turn to, they're saying the same things about the same events. It's downright freaky. I think the news is a lot like the advice you get from people. It seems like they're all repeating each other. So I ask you: If you do what they say, is that charting new territory or adding more of the same? Don't get me wrong—I have advisors who I trust implicitly, but I make sure to take in what they say, put it through my own personal filters, and then make a decision. I look around and decide if I think everyone is getting the same advice, or if it's right for me. As my advisors can tell you, I often don't do as they say. I'm sure they find it frustrating, but sometimes you just gotta do the opposite.

I'm going to share with you an example that I know some of you will not like, especially if you are a speaker like me. A few years ago I joined an association, and the first question I'd get was, "Do you have a book?" At the time I did have *Bootcamp360 for Brides*, but I was no longer in the fitness business, and I had not yet put pen to paper about thinking sideways, so I would answer, "No, why?"

No joke, everyone would say, "Well, you have to have a book to be credible" or "No one will take you seriously if you don't have a book." I would nod my head and move on. Finally, after getting really fed up that everyone was talking from the same script, another person asked me the same question. This time I turned to the back of the room where there was a pile of books and I asked, "If all 150 of us in the room have a book, and all of the thousands of us across the country have a book, then how does having a book help me stand out?" I want to thank those people for reminding me that doing what everyone is doing just because everyone else is doing it is not the right thing to do.

I love books. I think when the time is right and you have a lot to say that you should absolutely type away. But the valuable lesson here is never do something just because that is what everyone is telling you to do. It will fail. Write a book when the time is right and you have a lot to say. I waited two more years and let my other endeavors stand out. You need to think through why you are doing something and whether it's going to get you the results you want. It was those conversations (and having my antennas up) that led me to invest my time and money into the creation of our creativi-tees, T-shirts that let you wear your sideways thinking on your sleeve. You'd better believe that when a meeting planner gets eight books and one T-shirt in the mail, they remember the T-shirt. I booked many speaking gigs simply because I did the opposite of everyone else.

Don't worry about what everyone else is doing. Just because it's the "industry standard" doesn't mean it has to be yours. In fact, if someone tells you "that's the way it's always been done," then it should be your first clue to run the other way.

Let the QR Code take you to the download.

www.imaginibbles.com/think-sideways-playbook/

a game-changing playbook for disruptive thinking

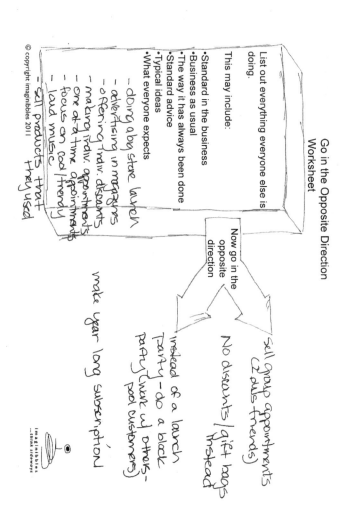

Go in the Opposite Direction
Worksheet

List out everything everyone else is doing.

This may include:

•Standard in the business
•Business as usual
•The way it has always been done
•Standard advice
•Typical ideas
•What everyone expects

– Doing a big store launch
– advertising in magazines
– offering indiv. discounts
– making indiv. appointments
– one at a time appointments
– focus on cool/trendy
– loud music
– sell products that they used

Now go in the opposite direction

sell group appointments (2 plus friends)

No discounts / gift bags instead

Instead of a launch party – do a block party (wine w/ others – pool customers)

make year long subscription

Think Sideways

Seize Change

My client and colleague Sam Johnston is a great example of seizing change. She is the executive director of the Colorado Press Association. As you can imagine, the press world is struggling. The decline in newspaper readership combined with the popularity of social media and mobile lifestyles has made many of their ways of thinking irrelevant. The newspaper industry is at odds with how the world has shifted. New models like Huffington-post.com, a news website and content-aggregating blog, Twitter, which allows you to communicate and share in 140 characters or less, and the 24-hour news cycle have greatly shifted people's expectations and habits. The news is no longer a one-way medium. We each experience the news differently. Some of you sit down with a cup of coffee and a paper, others read the news on your phones, and some do a mix of everything. All of this has shaken the foundation of the press world. As with any industry tipping point, a few brave souls see the future and seize it, while the majority fight to find a way to keep the old approach relevant. Unfortunately, the ones who fight the hardest are usually the ones who lose the most.

Sam said in a meeting, "Tradition is what got us here, but convention is what is holding us back." Sam recognizes that it's the traditions that made them successful, but in today's ever-changing world, holding on to old conventions is what is holding them back. Being able to recognize the difference between tradition and convention is difficult. It takes both perspective and vision. The Sideways Thinker knows when it's time to let go of how you did things and make room for new ways of thinking.

The mistake I see many individuals making is trying to hold on for dear life to old ways of thinking. Innovation doesn't come from fighting change, but from seizing it and grabbing it by the horns.

a game-changing playbook for disruptive thinking

Take Anythink library as an example. I know what you are thinking. Libraries are a place where you get "shhh'd" any time you speak above a whisper. You walk in quietly, check out a few books quietly, and leave quietly. While libraries have stayed relatively the same, the world around them has changed. Google is now our go-to source for any and all information. You can pretty much find an answer to anything online—trust me I've tried. Wikipedia, the online collaborative encyclopedia, is a go-to source whether you are satisfying your curiosity or researching a term paper. We catch the news on our mobiles and crowd-source answers to questions. I ask you, does a big building that warehouses books and tells you to "please be quiet" if you laugh out loud sound relevant? My kids and I spend a lot of time in libraries, and it feels like they are fighting the world and insisting that their old model is still meaningful.

Not Anythink libraries. They seized and harnessed the change around them. As the name suggests, it's less of a library and more of a community center where you are invited to unleash your imagination and engage your curiosity. They have employees called "wranglers," and when you walk through their doors you can feel the excitement. More importantly, you can hear it. There are people everywhere—and they're talking!

Even their website feels different. If you click on the Anythink Tank you'll find:

> What traditional conventions do you see at your library and how would you like to disrupt them? From "shhh" to Dewey Decimal to puppet shows, there are many stereotypes or "conventions" that seemingly define libraries in our industry and in the public's eye. What are some of the conventions you would like to disrupt so libraries remain relevant and vital to your community? How would you disrupt them?

Think Sideways

They actually encourage debate and ideas for disrupting their own category. That's bold! Even better, when people comment on this post, Anythink actually responds. Yes, they are listening.

They have gotten rid of the Dewey Decimal system and created libraries that look and feel more like cozy bookstores. There are fireplaces and portable furniture. As Pam Smith, the Executive Director, told me, "Anythink is so dynamic that it has a life of its own." They are true innovators in a struggling industry because they asked how they could embrace change.

It would have been very easy for Anythink to go down fighting. When they began this journey they were the least funded library system in Colorado per capita. But they defied the odds and are now a beacon of innovation and success. In fact, they are so passionate about spreading the word about innovation in libraries that they set up a conference called R-Squared, where librarians and administrators from across Colorado learn about transformation and innovation in libraries.

a game-changing playbook for disruptive thinking

Lean In

I was leading an innovation summit with a major advertising agency and their client, an alcohol beverage company. The room was full of a mix of people, some excited to be there and others who were skeptical that we would accomplish anything. One of the participants turned to his teammates and said something that I thought very wise:

> *"It's your job to lean in today. To be open and receptive. If you are leaning out, closed off, it's your fault."*

Leaning in tells the world, and more importantly yourself, that you are open to new ideas, engaged, participating in the world around you. Are you leaning forward on the edge of your seat, eyes wide open? Or are you that person who is sitting in the back, arms crossed, leaning back, telling the world you're not interested (jump to Eternal Optimism).

Great sideways thinkers are always leaning in. Every conversation, every experience is a chance for you to lean in. So check your posture, check your words. *Lean in.*

Create New Rules

Ask any college student who Johnny Cupcakes is and they'll tell you that he is this really cool guy that's all about lifestyle and living your dreams.

Johnny Earle, better known as "Johnny Cupcakes," is beloved because of his groundbreaking apparel business. His logo is a skull and crossbones, but the skull is in the shape of a cupcake. He was voted #1 Best Entrepreneur 25 and Under in 2008 by *Businessweek* magazine. His business is growing exponentially and he has some of the most loyal followers I've ever seen. I'm not kidding when I tell you that I saw a post on his Facebook Page with a picture of a shelving unit one of his customers had built to house the 300 Johnny Cupcakes shirts she owns.

Technically, Johnny Cupcakes is in the apparel business, but if you look closely, I think he runs his business more like a rock band on tour.

First, all his T-shirts are limited editions, like rock concert T-shirts. Second, he has his own brick and mortar shops. Walking into one of his stores is a total experience, like going to a rock concert. Third, he travels around the county speaking to college students with a message of opportunity and entrepreneurship. He also does road stops were he sells and signs T-shirts at local cupcake shops. Again, like a rock band on tour.

While all the other apparel companies are following the old rules of business, Johnny Cupcakes is making up his own rules. It's why he is thriving while others struggle to survive.

Making up your own rules can take many forms. It could be ignoring industry norms, like Johnny Cupcakes does. Or it could be choosing to break through rules that someone else laid down.

In fourth grade I was given the best homework a ten year old could possibly get. The teacher asked us to go home over the weekend and think about what we wanted to be when we grew up. On Monday we were to come in and present our decision to the class. I was so excited. I went running home, burst into the kitchen, and told my mom, "Cancel all playdates, I've got work to do!" (OK, not sure I had playdates, but I was a dramatic kid.) I spent the entire weekend writing down, erasing, and writing again the answer to that question. By Sunday night I had nailed it.

Monday I was the first to school, the first to my seat, and the first to raise my hand. I stood up in front of the dusty green chalkboard looking out at the sea of classmates sitting at those low chairs and tables. I mustered up all my confidence and said, "When I grow up I want to be President of the United States of America." And then I looked down at my shoes waiting for the obvious applause that was about to overtake my classmates. Instead of applause, I heard laughter.

Think Sideways

When I looked to the teacher for the save I realized that she was the one laughing. She stood and said, "Oh Tamara, you can't be President, you weren't born in this country and that's the rules, so go home and find a new dream."

I was crushed. I dragged my feet all the way home. When I got home my dad was working in his home office. I went in and asked him if my teacher was correct.

Without blinking an eye or even looking up from his work, my dad said, "Yes, that's the rule."

Now I'm really mad. I'm never speaking to my teacher or my dad ever again.

As I was huffing out of his office my dad looked up and said, "Tamara, if you don't like it, change the rules."

I've never forgotten that lesson. It's true that I have dual citizenship, but I wasn't born on US soil. Now that I'm an adult, I'm not sure I'd want that job. But what I've realized since is that rules can be changed, and how you accomplish your goals can be changed. Instead of being President and making a difference that way, I give to charity both through my business and personally.

So the next time someone tells you that you can't do something because "That's the rules," go write the rule in pencil, erase the parts you don't like, and fill them in with something that works better for you.

Get Emotional

We work so hard to leave our emotional sides at home when we step out into the work world. Somewhere along the way we were told that being emotional is immature and childish and serves no purpose in business.

  "Never apologize 4 showing feeling. When u do so, you apologize for the truth." Benjamin Disraeli

What if I told you that, in your emotions, you'll find empathy and creativity? It is said that Steve Jobs cried when he watched the breakthrough Apple ad from the 1984 Super Bowl. We are emotional creatures living in emotional times. In Daniel Pink's book *A Whole New Mind: Why Right-Brainers Will Rule the Future* (Riverhead Trade, 2006), he talks about the fact that we've shifted from an information age built on sequential logic and information to a conceptual age built on empathy and emotion. People are naturally emotional. We seek to connect on an emotional level; we make decisions based on emotion. Think about the last time you bought something—your shampoo, a cell phone, some workout gear. I bet you'll find that emotions drive a lot of your purchasing decisions (jump to Write a Manifesto). I know they do mine.

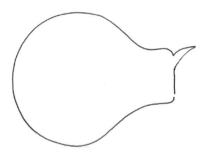

Think Sideways

Do a little test. Write down your three favorite brands, then write down why you buy them. If you ask me about my favorites—Puma, Apple, SmashBurger—I would say I like things that are innovative, sleek, funky, and clever. I could probably get footwear anywhere, but I don't. I could buy any mobile device, but I never will. I could have a decent burger and sweet potato fries in most restaurants, but I try not to. It's not that I'm highly loyal. In fact, there is nothing I love more than trying new products. But these brands do a fantastic job of connecting with me on an emotional level.

In a keynote speech "The Science of Emotion," Antonio R. Damasio, M.D., Ph.D, M.W. Van Allen Professor and Head of the Department of Neurology at the University of Iowa College of Medicine, and adjunct professor at the Salk Institute in La Jolla, California, said:

> *"Emotion is an adaptive response, part of the vital process of normal reasoning and decision-making. It is one of the highest levels of bio-regulation for the human organism and has an enormous influence on the maintenance of our homeostatic balance and thus of our well-being. Last but not least, emotion is critical to learning and memory."*

Don't be afraid to get emotional. It's how we operate, so why would we avoid it in our work?

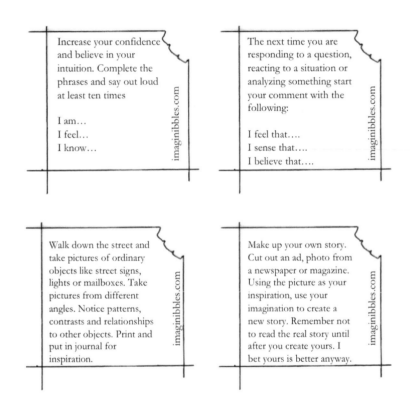

Increase your confidence and believe in your intuition. Complete the phrases and say out loud at least ten times

I am...
I feel...
I know...

imaginibbles.com

The next time you are responding to a question, reacting to a situation or analyzing something start your comment with the following:

I feel that....
I sense that....
I believe that....

imaginibbles.com

Walk down the street and take pictures of ordinary objects like street signs, lights or mailboxes. Take pictures from different angles. Notice patterns, contrasts and relationships to other objects. Print and put in journal for inspiration.

imaginibbles.com

Make up your own story. Cut out an ad, photo from a newspaper or magazine. Using the picture as your inspiration, use your imagination to create a new story. Remember not to read the real story until after you create yours. I bet yours is better anyway.

imaginibbles.com

Think Sideways

a game-changing playbook for disruptive thinking

Hi there, I'm Col Laberate...

I am a super hero and people are drawn to me. I am naturally magnetic, pulling people towards my gravitational pull. Once you are near me I can bring out the best in you and make you want to work with others for a common good. You can't help but want to be near me. When I smile you will be transformed into an action-oriented, collaborative person. I warn you, no one can escape my undeniable magnetism. My team will be the one you want to be on.

a game-changing playbook for disruptive thinking

Hi, I'm Noah Action...

I am a super villain and I have the ability to make you stop what you are doing dead in your tracks. It's as if I freeze all momentum and even stop time. Because of me nothing gets past the idea stage, and I like it that way. I can erase people's minds and implant unimportant things to do that will have you spinning your wheels all day. If you come near me, your ideas will get trapped and eventually disappear.

a game-changing playbook for disruptive thinking

SIDEWAYS

EXERCISES

www.imaginibbles.com/think-sideways-playbook/

You diligently set your alarm clock to go off at five in the morning so you can drag yourself to the gym. Or maybe over lunch you pop out to go for a quick run. Or perhaps you are one of the millions of people who have home exercise equipment. You could be one of many who make it to the gym once a month and then pull something in your leg because you overdo it. This isn't a fitness book, and everyone knows I've been each of those people at different stages of my life.

I've come to realize that what I put into my fitness regimen is what I get out of it. If I exercise daily, by the time the weekend rolls around I'm easily hiking up that mountainside. When I skip my fitness program for a few weeks, those hikes don't go so well. I eventually get to the top, but I'm huffing and puffing more than usual.

To maintain your fitness level you have to give your body consistent exercise and nutritious fuel. The sideways mind works the same way. You can either let it collect dust in a drawer, pulling it out for the occasional creative endeavor while huffing and puffing through it, or you can do daily exercises that maintain and even strengthen your mental and imaginative fitness. That's what this segment is all about. Easy-to-do, simple-to-incorporate exercises that help you reach your creative potential.

This is another part of the playbook you can whip open at any time—while working in a café, at your kitchen table, during a big meeting, or while collaborating in your office. These exercises work great solo or with a crowd. Just like physical fitness, each exercise works your brain in a slightly different way for a whole-mind workout. I equate it to those parcourses we did as kids. Do you remember those? You'd go hiking and along the way you'd see and maybe do those weird stations.

Some were for sit-ups, others for plyometrics, and some just looked like weird torture contraptions. By the time you were done you had worked out your body in multiple ways. They always made me sore in places I didn't even know I had muscles.

If you are stuck, whip out the playbook and get unstuck. If you're looking to start the day by revving up your creative metabolism, pick an exercise and do it for 10 minutes. Break up your routine with an exercise or end it on a creative high note.

You'll instantly feel more creative, and in one week you'll notice some definition in your creative muscles. After 90 days you'll be bench-pressing ideas like it's nothing. Don't wait until Monday to get going (unless today is Monday).

Ask

On average, Preschool children ask their parents 100 questions a day. If you're a parent like me, you know what it's like. "Why is the sky blue?" "Why do dogs have four legs?" "How can dad hear you through a phone?" "How does the doorbell work?" They think about everything we take for granted as adults and question it all, even the most obvious.

Somewhere along the way we stopped asking and started assuming we know the answer. You need to get back to being crazy-curious (jump to Lean In). Asking forces you to challenge the rules. What are the rules anyway? Most of the time they are someone else's way of doing things. But that doesn't mean they have to be yours. Every time you think you know the answer, ask another question. Every time you think something is set in stone, ask, "Why?" If something is considered a given, ask, "What if?" It's when we see the world through inquisitive eyes that we begin to see innovative ideas.

Ed Goodman, chief experience officer of Spiral Experiences, used to be an "Imagineer" at Disney. I confess, I'm a little jealous. That's the ultimate sideways-thinking job. As a Disney Imagineer, your job responsibility, even your job title, includes being imaginative. It's like the Navy Seals of creativity. Ed and six other Imagineers were tasked with coming up with a new parade for Disneyland, a parade that would wow adults and delight little children. If you've ever been to one of the Disney parks as a child, taken your kids, had a neighbor who went, or just watched the commercials on TV, you know that the bar has been set incredibly high. To come up with a parade that exceeds current experiences is a daunting task. But, these are Imagineers, and it's their job to wow.

Wrong questions don't shut down ideas, wrong assumptions and answers do

Seven of them sat around a conference room table, coming up with an idea here and there, but nothing with much wow factor. It's getting down to the wire and now they're worried. The deadline is fast approaching and all they have to show for it are empty pizza boxes, stale coffee, and walls filled with uninspired notes on easel pads. On the final day, one of the Imagineers brings in his young daughter, hoping that having a child's perspective will lead to great idea. Much to the Imagineers' dismay, this eight-year-old is more interested in her juice boxes and coloring books. The day wears on and still, nothing. After lunch, the little girl raises her hand and asks:

"Why do parades have to be on the ground?"

And with that one question, the Imagineers went running to the whiteboard to create a parade like no other, with lights in the sky and balloons and wheels. That little girl had something more powerful than an answer—she had a question. That one question challenged the simple assumption that parades are always on the ground. With that one knock over the head, the Imagineers were able to break free from tradition and take the parade to new heights.

Practice the art of asking every day.

Ask why. Ask what if.

Think Sideways

Why does a toothbrush have bristles?
What if books were watched, not read?
What if socks didn't have to match?
What if yoga was a hard-core exercise?

Asking that last question led Trevor Tice to create Core-Power Yoga, an intense yoga practice for athletes based on the ancient principals of yoga, but often set to pop music and mixed up with core work. Tice wanted more hard-core athletes and weekend warriors to experience the benefits of yoga but knew that, for that to happen, it couldn't only be about meditation. Now, I'm not saying I don't enjoy a few minutes of Corpse Pose at the end, but wow, do you work hard to even get there. CorePower Yoga also took it one step further, and asked why yoga studios had to be individually owned and operated. Did you notice how five years ago, yoga studios were these little niche studios? Instead, CorePower Yoga blended all the benefits of your local yoga studio with a great business concept. They now have more than 55 studios, and are still growing. Their members are die-hard and expect a killer workout along with some mental cleansing. I know when I travel I seek out CorePower Yoga studios because, like Starbucks, I know it's going to be a consistent experience everywhere I go.

Ask, ask, and ask some more. Never be afraid to ask. Follow the QR Code for the Ask worksheet.

www.imaginibbles.com/think-sideways-playbook/

a game-changing playbook for disruptive thinking

Ask Worksheet

What if a tooth brush didn't have bristles?
What if books were watched, not read?
What if socks didn't have to match?
What if yoga was a hard core exercise?
Why do I have to take this next step?
Why does it always work this way?
Why can't I do it differently?

Exercise:

Write down one rule or assumption in your world.
Ex: I have to invest a lot of money to get my business going.

need beautiful brochures, marketing materials for sales

Now write down with a What If or Why as if the opposite were true.
Ex: Why do I have to invest a lot of money to get my business going?
What if I can do this grassroots?

what if everything was online?
what if I didn't need marketing materials?

Ideate off of the Why and What If questions...

– Spend more energy getting people to come as guests
– offer a trial/demo instead of paper that gets thrown in trash
– ask for a conversation

Think Sideways

Break

If you work at Google, you get 20% of your time to work on whatever project you wish. I'm not talking after-hours or week-ends. I'm talking 20% of your Monday through Friday work time is reserved for you to explore your own ideas. It sounds like a luxury, but Google recognizes that giving people time away from their day-to-day tasks benefits the individual and the company. It was a few guys playing around in their 20% who created Google Maps, an app that none of us can live without.

  Do you really think staring at your computer screen will help? Go fly a kite or cook a 3-course meal.

Breaking can take lots of forms. It can be a mental break, a physical break, or something that encompasses both. A break can be a few minutes, a few hours, or even a few days.

The next time you feel like you are banging your head against the wall, give yourself permission to just walk away. Go to a class at the gym, call a friend, follow a rabbit hole online. Sometimes you just need to take a break from the day-to-day to give your sideways thinking a chance to engage. It's when we create that mental space that our imagination kicks into high gear. It may not be conscious, but amazing things are happening. It gives your mind some much-needed breathing room. It's actually OK to leave things unfinished. You may come back with an even better idea. Don't let the need to cross one more thing off your to-do list get in the way of more creative output.

Here are a few other ways to take a break:

Doodle, go for a walk around the block, watch a movie, stretch, play a game on your iPhone, play foursquare at the playground, grab a cup of coffee, meditate, do a random search online, journal, play with LEGOs, cook, clean a room, take a drive in a new neighborhood, work on something totally different, shop online, get a glass of water, talk to a stranger, watch a funny video online.

I reserve half a day every week to break free from my immediate tasks. Some of my best ideas, like the inspiration for imagi-NATION™, have come from those breaks.

Play

It's silly, it's fun, and it increases your ability to think sideways. Play increases your curiosity, which leads to a greater sense of discovery, which ultimately leads to creativity.

According to The Strong, an educational institution dedicated to the study of play, play is critical to human development, including the development of creativity, problem solving, and resilience. Research shows that play fosters curiosity, discovery, and openness; all key factors for thinking sideways. (Discover The Strong and the National Museum of Play http://ow.ly/9hZ5i)

Clearly, engaging in play does a lot of things, but let me focus on a few that I think have a direct effect on thinking sideways.

First, play puts you at ease. When you are playing you aren't as worried about the consequences. It's just playing around after all, and when you aren't thinking about the consequences you are more open to disruptive ideas. Also, when you aren't worried about the consequences you are more likely to take risks.

Think about the last time you played *Monopoly*. You probably took that risk and put a hotel on Boardwalk. It's fun to play. Play makes you happy, and you all know that a happy person is a more creative person. It's hard to be creative when you are down in the dumps. You don't have to turn everything into a game to get the benefits of play. Think about how it makes you feel. You feel curious; you are receptive and open to having fun. Infusing just tiny elements of play into your business culture can have the same effect.

When I'm doing an innovation training, I place random toys on each person's chair. I encourage people to sculpt the Play-Doh or build with blocks. I know that when they do those things they are more likely to be open-minded and listen to what I have to say. They are having fun. It's also good to know that people who report having fun while they learn show a higher rate of retention. So if you want people to remember what you are saying, make it playful.

Play is more than board games or cops and robbers. It's about adding play to everyday moments. If you've ever worked with me you know that I love whipping out toy microphones during meetings that have gotten a little heavy. It's not because I want to stop discussions that need to happen, it's because I know that getting people to laugh helps put them at ease and lets them engage with each other. It makes people more receptive to other's ideas and pushback. Of course, if you feel the need to ride down a slide or bounce on a trampoline, don't let me stop you.

You'll often find me at my kids' school, engaging in a killer game of foursquare with my sons. My creative endorphins are released and I'm in a much happier mood when I sit down at my desk to tackle my to-do list.

I'm sure you've noticed that my title isn't "President" or "Founder," it's "Chief Imaginator." Play can be everywhere. If you call the imaginarium and get our voicemail, you'll hear a message that goes something like:

> *"Thank you for calling imaginibbles. Please leave your name, number, a brief message, and tell us who would play you in a movie about your life."*

Play can be everywhere. Check out Funtheory.com and the fun theory award, an initiative by Volkswagen. Kevin Richardson, the winner, set out to prove that you change human behavior by making things fun. He transformed a set of relatively unused stairs coming out of a subway station into a piano keyboard. Once the piano was in place, people actually stopped taking the escalator and started taking the stairs. Fun can do wonders for your willingness to complete a task.

Fun theory piano video: http://ow.ly/94pIe

 Random idea #88773 Headsets where you digitally load up the songs you want for your workout. This way you don't have to mess with wires. Maybe voice activated to go forward and back if you want to skip or repeat a song.

Smash

Alton Brown grew up with passion and flair for cooking. As an adult, he didn't immediately follow his passions, but he spent a decade as a TV studio cameraman instead. Between shoots, Alton would sneak off the set and watch the cooking shows being shot in other studios.

Even though he loved food, he found the cooking shows to be dull and boring. At that time they all looked alike—a chef standing perfectly behind a counter covered with pre-chopped ingredients laid out perfectly in bowls, pots hanging perfectly overhead, and flowers arranged perfectly in the background. A few chops, a few dices and—tah-dah!—a perfectly prepared meal pops out of the fake oven.

Alton promised himself that if he ever had a cooking show of his own it would be a mix of Julia Child, Mr. Wizard, and Monty Python. He fulfilled that promise by going on to become the inspiration and host of *Good Eats*, which ran for 13 consecutive years. If you've ever seen it, you know that it's this weird mix of pop culture, food science, and good food. It's like no other cooking show, which is one of the reasons it has been so successful for so many years.

Check out his website at http://ow.ly/96ePB

Alton Brown, when given the opportunity to create his own show, didn't follow in the footsteps of other television chefs. Alton smashed together three seemingly random concepts to create a completely new cooking show experience.

a game-changing playbook for disruptive thinking

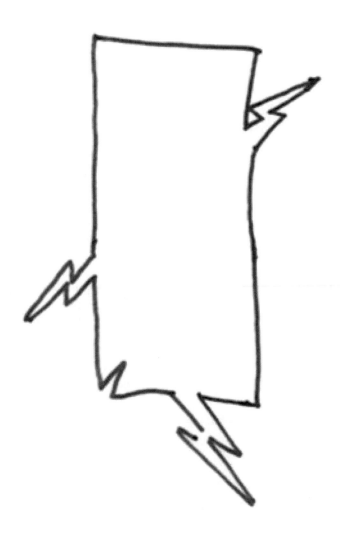

Think Sideways

When my team is working through a problem, I often ask how they'd solve it in a completely different category. Our Daily Dose exercise cards are the result of smashing together bookmarks and fitness programs. Why those two, you ask? We knew we wanted a product that acted as a daily reminder to unleash creativity.

What two random things do that well? Bookmarks and fitness programs. Bookmarks make their way to the fridge door, by your computer, or into the book you are reading. You see them daily. Easy, at-home fitness programs break down a daunting task into bite-size exercises you can do daily. Smash those two seemingly random things together and you get this.

  Innovation happens at the intersection of random – Medici Effect (great book)

a game-changing playbook for disruptive thinking

Smashing is a great tool when you feel like you're stuck in a rut. You can truly smash anything together and come up with new ideas. It's impossible not to. Let's practice:

Smash together these random things and see what new ideas you come up with.

Ask yourself:

What do these two things have in common?
If I smash these two things together, what ideas come to mind?
If I were to merge these two things, what would happen?

Popcorn and a rainbow
Mobile phone and a hotel
Wine bottle and home décor

Here is your worksheet for smashing whatever you are working on with random objects. Download the full-size worksheet by following the QR Code.

www.imaginibbles.com/think-sideways-playbook/

Ideas at the Intersection of Random Worksheet

My burning question: how do I capture/reach college market with my products?

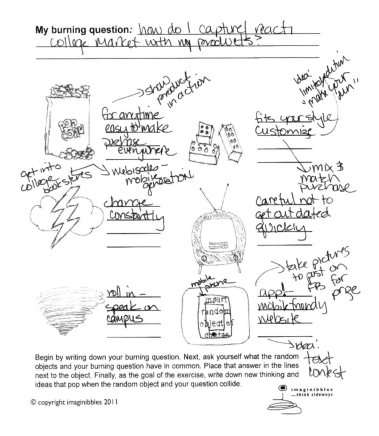

For anytime
easy to make
purchase
everywhere

→ show product in action

get into college bookstores → webisodes – mobile generation

change constantly

roll in – speak on campus

mobile phone

insert random object of choice

Idea: limited edition "make your own"

fits your style
customize

→ mix & match purchase

careful not to get outdated quickly

→ take pictures to post on FB for prize

app! mobile-friendly website

→ idea: text contest

Begin by writing down your burning question. Next, ask yourself what the random objects and your burning question have in common. Place that answer in the lines next to the object. Finally, as the goal of the exercise, write down new thinking and ideas that pop when the random object and your question collide.

imaginibbles
...think sideways

© copyright imaginibbles 2011

a game-changing playbook for disruptive thinking

Throw Away

It's easy to fall in love with mediocre ideas. They're usually the first we think of and they masquerade as "easy opportunities" or "low-hanging fruit." Sometimes our first ideas are good ones, but what if you were forced to keep on thinking? What if you couldn't use your first idea?

Whenever I'm working on a new product concept, I like to throw away my first ten ideas. I act as if the idea wasn't good enough, crumple it up, and toss it into a small box on the table. Like shampoo and conditioner, I rinse and repeat. Throwing my ideas away convinces my brain that whatever I came up with, it wasn't good enough, so now I have to stretch a bit further. With the crumpling of each idea my creativity gets wilder. When I'm all done, I dump all the crumpled pages out on the desk, un-crumple them, and explore what I wrote. Usually I find that the winning idea is a combination of something I wrote down on the first and final pieces of paper.

"One's mind once stretched by a new idea, never regains its original dimensions."
- Oliver Wendell Holmes

To get a wastebasket full of ideas, have others do this with you. Don't underestimate the power of physically throwing the ideas away. It's an important part of the process. Each idea must be written or drawn on separate pieces of paper and thrown into the waste bucket. No exceptions.

Step one: place multiple pieces of blank paper & pens on your desk.
Step two: place a wastebasket or box in the middle of the desk.
Step three: write or sketch an idea on a piece of paper.
Step four: crumple it up & throw it in the wastebasket on the desk.
Step five: repeat at least ten times.

Follow the QR Code to download these instructions.

www.imaginibbles.com/think-sideways-playbook/

a game-changing playbook for disruptive thinking

Throw Ideas Away Worksheet

Step one: place multiple pieces of blank paper and pens on your desk
Step two: place a wastebasket or box in the middle of the desk
Step three: write or sketch your idea on a piece of paper
Step four: crumple it up and throw it in the wastebasket on your desk
Step five: repeat at least ten times

Finally, pull all the crumpled up pieces of paper out of the wastebasket.
Lay out on desk and explore

Think Sideways

Say Yes

Nothing makes you die a little bit inside more than that inter-action with the "Yes-But" guy. You know who he is. The one who objects to every idea. He starts every sentence with, "Yes, but," "That won't work because," or "Here's the challenge with that…" You turn left down the hallway just to avoid him. Yes-But is a killer of sideways thinking. It keeps the momentum from ever getting rolling, and keeps people from putting their sideways hat on.

According to emotional intelligence expert, speaker, educator, and author Scott Halford:

> *"The brain builds new neural pathways out of 'yes' not 'no.' You can't 'don't' yourself into a new behavior. Think 'can' not 'can't'"*

The brain doesn't stretch by using Yes-But language. If you ever visit the imaginarium you'll find a few Yes-But jars. If you start a sentence with any "Yes, but" statements, you have to put money in the jar. I've enjoyed a few lattes thanks to that jar (jump to Play). What I really want is for that jar to be empty. Having a Yes-But jar reminds you not to become that guy. It gives you permission to call out that guy that keeps shooting down every idea.

If you need to squelch the Yes-But jerk, set the group up for success by having a Yes-And conversation. Yes-And con-versations have the opposite effect. Yes-And builds momentum and encourages people to put on their sideways-thinking caps. It's a tried-and-true trick that I've learned along the way. It's great for setting the tone of a conversation or meeting.

Here's how it works as an exercise:

Start by deciding what you are going to build. It could be an energy drink or an athletic shoe or a new rocket ship. Anything goes. Get the group to stand up and move around. Movement is important for this exercise, so make sure the team has room to roam as they talk. The rules are simple. First, you must start your statement by saying, "Yes, and it…" Once someone says something, it is cast in stone. So if I say that the energy drink is in a purple can, the next person can't say, "Or it's in a brown can." They can say, "Yes, and it has brown wings." The next person might say, "Yes, and it refills itself."

I often use this exercise to warm up a group before dealing with the real issues. It gets everyone in the right mindset.

People usually start out relatively subdued, but eventually the crazy things come out. I once heard a woman say, "Yes, and the rocket ship makes martinis when you hit the outer atmosphere."

A few minutes of this exercise and you and your team will be ready to have a sideways conversation infused with new thinking and laughter. In some ways, it's like a safe place to practice wild and crazy thinking, and it preps you to do more of it in real life.

To do this with a group, all you have to do is first chose something to build, and then lay down the ground rules mentioned above.

1. Anything goes
2. You have to start your build with, "Yes, and"
3. Once someone says something it is set in stone

On a side note, you can also do this one by yourself. Follow your own train of thought, starting each build with a Yes-And bubble.

Follow the QR Code for the full page version of this worksheet.

www.imaginibbles.com/think-sideways-playbook/

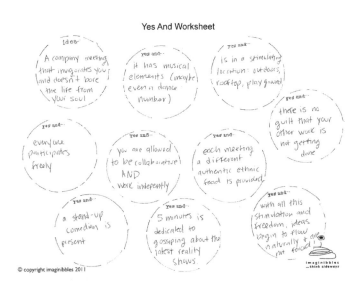

a game-changing playbook for disruptive thinking

Look at this on a personal level as well. There is a big difference between Yes-And people and Yes-But people. Think about your friends. You can probably call out who are the momentum builders and who are the momentum killers. The momentum killers suck the life out of you. They often leave you feeling insecure and doubting your disruptive dreams. Get rid of them! I know it's hard to do, but Yes-But-ers do nothing but bring you down. If you are truly serious about unleashing your disruptive dreamer with sideways thinking, then it's time to walk away from those who deplete your dreams. Instead, surround yourself with Yes-And people.

They're the ones who will support you, shower you with random ideas, and help you take it to the next level. They are the people that make you feel wiser and better for having spent time with them. Think about who you are surrounded by. If you walk away from an encounter saying, "Well that was a waste of an hour," then it's time to let that person go. If you walk away saying, "That was totally awesome," then they're a keeper. I know this might sound harsh, but life is too short to be surrounded by sinkers when there are so many rockets willing to lift you up.

"Creativity for the joy of others is the greatest delight. Oh what fun it is to help people feel most alive."
- Giovanni Livera

Follow a Mutation

You may not know the name Judson Laippley, but I bet you are one of the more than 188 million people who have viewed his video "The Evolution of Dance" on YouTube. Judson was a public speaker who had achieved moderate success, but one little mutation changed his path and his trajectory. After speaking to a group of college students, which included his performance of "The Evolution of Dance," one of the students followed up and asked Judson if he wouldn't mind putting the video on YouTube so that the student and his friends could learn it. Judson, honored that someone wanted to learn his dance routine, agreed, but had no idea how to go about it. The college kid told him how to post it on YouTube.

Judson had no idea what this YouTube thing was, but he agreed to figure it out. YouTube was only nine months old at the time, but it was so easy to use that Judson figured it out and posted "The Evolution of Dance" online. A few days later his friends were calling him. "Dude, did you know thousands of people have watched your video?" Judson was amazed. He would log on and literally watch the views ticker shoot up. When it hit one million he was amazed. The views grew exponentially, landing him appearances on everything from *The Ellen DeGeneres Show* to the *Today* show on NBC.

Judson and I had some very interesting conversations. What struck me wasn't how clever his dance is—and it is clever—but how he followed a mutation. The success of his video was a trifecta of a college student's request, a new video sharing technology, and a funny dance. Kabam! A major mutation. Many people would watch in awe at their own success and end up with a one-hit wonder. Not Judson. As a Sideways Thinker Judson jumped on that mutation and turned it into a highly successful business.

a game-changing playbook for disruptive thinking

"The Evolution of Dance" has turned into keynote speeches, books, CDs, and more. Judson couldn't have anticipated that this mutation would happen. We never can, but we can identify and harness them when they do.

Pay close attention. Mutations are bound to happen, but it's up to you to seize them like Judson did. When you see something that seems like an anomaly or a rare occurrence, follow it. You never know where that mutation can take you. I think Judson would tell you that despite the business plans and well thought-out strategy, the dance mutation was the best thing that ever happened to his business. See "The Evolution of Dance" at http://ow.ly/8JQzF

  Random idea #034834 – little gadget that keeps ur car cool in summer. Plugs into lighter, uses minimal energy to keep air cool so when get in don't burn butt on seats.

A mutation may be something huge or a minor offshoot. It could be a shift in your business direction or taking note of a wildly successful marketing campaign. Use this sheet to keep track of the mutations. Mind-map off of them how you might harness them for success. Click on the QR Code for this fantastic worksheet.

www.imaginibbles.com/think-sideways-playbook/

Think Sideways

3 133

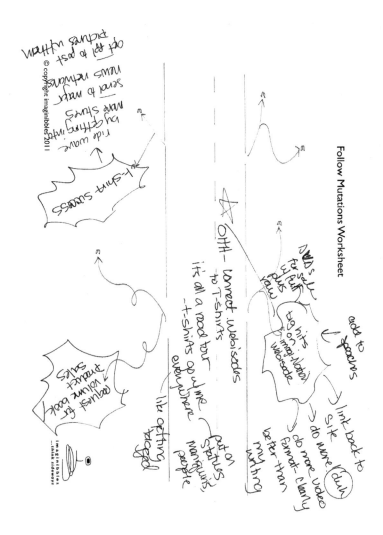

Follow Mutations Worksheet

Go Wide

They say that great innovators simply have more dots to connect. So, lesson here, go get more dots. It's one thing to go deep, but I'd suggest that to get more dots to connect, go wide. Expand your knowledge far beyond your current world. I'm not asking you to become an expert in anything. Actually, I'm asking you not to. Instead, I want you to go far and wide with your knowledge. That's how you gather a lot of dots to connect. Life offers many chances to expand your knowledge:

- Type in a famous person's name on Wikipedia.com
- Watch a video on Ted.com
- Read a random magazine at the grocery store
- Watch an episode of imagi-NATION™
- Take a class on something you've never done, like sewing or snowboarding
- Listen to talk radio in your car
- Ask a friend to explain something they are knowledgeable about to you

One of my best sideways ideas came from reading an article in a magazine about dirt bike racing, which is something in which I have no experience or interest. The article talked about how dirt bikers have their own language. They have phrases and words for everything, and it's that language that makes them an interwoven community. Connecting that dot of knowledge with my work helped me coin the phrase Think Sideways and transform it from something I used occasionally to a common phrase that unites innovators, disruptors, and creatives. We all think sideways.

Learn something about a new sport, skill or technique. Go to eHow.com or search on Google. If you know how to ski look for a video on knitting. If you know how to knit, look for a video on yoga. Lose your mind in something new.

imaginibbles.com

In Feng Shui it is believed that a lucky bamboo can bring health, wealth and happiness. Go buy a bamboo plant and write down five things you feel fortune for in this world. Giving thanks brings more fortune.

imaginibbles.com

The next time you are in line or waiting your turn somewhere, strike up a conversation with a stranger. You'll learn something new every time. Ask questions like:
What was the best part of today?
How is your day going

imaginibbles.com

Expand your mind by reading a new magazine. Pick one outside of your knowledge set, hobbies or lifestyle. Cut out interesting facts, images and articles for your journal.

imaginibbles.com

a game-changing playbook for disruptive thinking

Creative Productivity

"Tamara, I loved the exercise you gave us around doodling. I felt the creativity oozing out of me but I have to say I was worried that my boss would come up behind me and say, 'What am I paying you for?'"

That was a comment from a person who attended one of my innovation seminars. I think what she said reflects the sad truth about business today. We worry so much about being visibly productive, checking off the tasks on our to-do list, that we've stopped valuing creative tasks. We measure someone's effort or accomplishments by how long they work. The guy that gets in before everyone else at 6:30 a.m. and is always the last one burning the midnight oil gets all the accolades for being a smart, dedicated worker. I see this across the spectrum, from small mom & pop shops to major global conglomerates. I think it's sad. It's sad that working long hours is more often rewarded than working smart.

In honor of guitar legend Les Paul, Google posted a guitar designed with the Google logo. The cool thing was that it allowed users to interactively strum the guitar. How fun is that! Apparently really fun. Over two days, millions of Google users also thought it was wicked cool. It's estimated that 10.7 million man-hours were spent strumming the Google guitar strings.

Very quickly, a statistic came out saying that $268 million dollars of productivity were lost because of all the hours spent jamming out on Google's guitar. (It was calculated based on the average salary in the United States.)

The part that struck me was "lost productivity." I'm not convinced that's how we should look at the time spent strumming away during work hours. In fact, I think we should initiate another study that shows the many great ideas, brilliant solutions, and new paths of thinking that came after a few minutes of creative play.

Play ignites the curious mind. It engages your sense of discovery and wonder, which in turn increases your creativity. So for that, I say, play away! Perhaps a few minutes of playful fun is exactly what you need to get those ideas flowing.

In fact, due to the popularity of the Google guitar, they've decided to give it a permanent home. Here is the link: www.google.com/logos/2011/lespaul.html. Go make some beautiful music! PS—hit record and let Google play back your musical genius.

Creative productivity is as important as task-driven productivity. In the 2010 IBM Global CEOs study, they found that CEOs ranked creativity as the most important crucial factor for success. Given the importance of creativity, isn't it time we actually allowed space for creative activities that foster sideways thinking?

Don't hesitate to venture off your to-do list and doodle, take a walk, or gossip about your favorite celebrity for a few minutes. I make sure that at least 20% of my work week is dedicated to creative productivity. Some weeks this is a series of five-minute blocks, and other weeks it may be a couple of hours or a full day. You'll find when you get back to your to-do list you'll be invigorated enough to tackle it with gusto. You'll get more done and do it without having to stay up until midnight because you'll work smarter and bring more innovative solutions to the table.

a game-changing playbook for disruptive thinking

Get Lost

Your brain is highly efficient. Once it knows how to do something, it creates shortcuts so that you operate with the least possible effort. It's how we get through life. It allows your brain to filter out all the insignificant details you encounter every day. Just think how overwhelming it would be if you took in every detail. You would go on overload. So the brain, being efficient, filters most of it out. You take in what you need and everything else goes unnoticed. However, have you ever noticed what happens when you get lost?

Let's say you decided to take a cross-country trip and you think you may have missed the exit to your hotel. Your brain recognizes that it doesn't have shortcuts, so its creative problem-solving side kicks in, and so does its ability to notice. Suddenly you notice the sun in relation to the mountains, and notice that you've passed that gas station with the red sign three times. You notice details, you take it all in, and you creatively put it all together to either determine where you are, or decide you need to ask someone for directions.

Getting lost mentally and physically makes you a little more curious (jump to Don't Step Outside Your Comfort Zone). You take in more details about your surroundings than you might normally. Getting lost creates new synapse connections as you make meaning out of your new environment. And when it comes to creativity, the more synapses the better.

- Explore a neighborhood you've never gone to.
- Drive a new route to work.
- Walk a different way to the store. It's easy to get lost if you veer off and step out of your routine.

Spontaneous Collaboration

Stop brainstorming! Oh I bet you never thought you'd hear me say that.

I think brainstorms kill creativity. In fact, I gave an entire Ignite speech on it to 800-some cheering audience members in Boulder, Colorado. I think they feel the same way.

Watch it at http://ow.ly/8JR46

Think about what your last brainstorm looked like. You all shuffled into the conference room at 2:00 p.m. and your host warmed you up with some clever icebreaker where you had to clap, smile, clap, and then pat your head. Next, they gave you the rules and what's out of bounds. Finally, you were broken into groups of three, armed with scented markers (aka corporate crack), and sent to opposite sides of the room to fill up easel sheets with ideas.

a game-changing playbook for disruptive thinking

You were expected to suddenly transform from a worker bee into a creative magician. By the end, you were supposed to have pulled ideas out of the hat like rabbits. More often than not, it doesn't work. I'm not saying there isn't a time and place to get together like this, but I am saying there is a better way—spontaneous collaboration. Spontaneous collaboration is people and ideas intersecting randomly all day.

Steve Jobs, in the MSNBC documentary about Pixar, was asked about their success. As you may recall, they had more than seven blockbuster hits in a row. It started with *Toy Story* in 1995 and went on to include *Monsters Inc.*, *Finding Nemo*, *The Incredibles, Up,* and several others you've probably seen. Their 11th film, *Toy Story III*, is the highest-grossing animated movie of all time, worldwide. Steve Jobs attributed part of their success to "unplanned collaboration" or spontaneous collaboration. In fact, he felt so strongly about it that when Pixar hit it big and they were looking to move out of their initial office, Jobs insisted that the new office design include an open courtyard to allow for spontaneous encounters that would lead to spontaneous collaboration.

Today, engage in these five spontaneous collaboration activities:

- If you work in an office, place a couple chairs in the hall.
- Stop anyone who walks by and ask for five minutes of their time to talk through your idea with you.
- Stay in the elevator for a few extra floors and talk to the people with you.
- Ask a random colleague to take the stairs with you so that the two of you can talk.
- If you're a solo-preneur, find a busy café and ask anyone who sits next to you for a few minutes of advice.
- If you are stuck in line at the mall, talk to a stranger about your idea.

One of my best ideas for how to bring a story to life for a keynote speech came from a random conversation I had with a stranger at the post office.

Idea-Cache

Idea-caching was born out my love for geo-caching. For those of you who have done it you know it's like a fun treasure hunt. Geo-caches are small containers filled with goodies and a log of those who've found them, hidden all across the globe—in cities, on hikes, and on the sides of volcanoes. You go to the website Geocaching.com and enter in a zip code or keyword search and find geo-caches in your area. You then get the latitude and longitude of the geo-cache and occasionally a few hints about how to find it. You grab a few trinkets and embark on a quest to find your geo-cache. I once searched and discovered a geo-cache on Table Mountain in Golden, Colorado.

I put in a LEGO guy and took out a plastic troll. According to the log, the troll had made its way to Colorado all the way from Switzerland. I then took the troll with me on a trip to Costa Rica and placed it in a geo-cache on a trail at the base of Arenal volcano.

Later, during a conversation with my idea-sharing buddy Gina Schreck from Synapse 3Di, I mumbled something like, "Hmmm, shouldn't ideas work like that? You give a little, you take a little. Something different in the cache every time so every time is a different experience."

After a very loud conversation with Gina we realized that yes, ideas can work like that. In fact, they often do work better like that, because you're infusing random and spontaneous responses to your ideas all day. Each time someone goes back to the mind-map it looks a little different, and because it looks different they come up with new ideas.

If you work in an office building, tape the following worksheet by the elevator, in the kitchen, or by the front door. Leave a bowl of pens next to it. In the center circle write one single idea, challenge, or opportunity you are working on. Then, let people randomly mind-map on your idea-caching sheet all day.

Eventually it will look something like this, with new ideas hitting the paper every time someone puts a pen to the idea-cache.

Follow the QR Code for a life-size version of this worksheet.

www.imaginibbles.com/think-sideways-playbook/

Idea-Cache Worksheet

Your ideas:

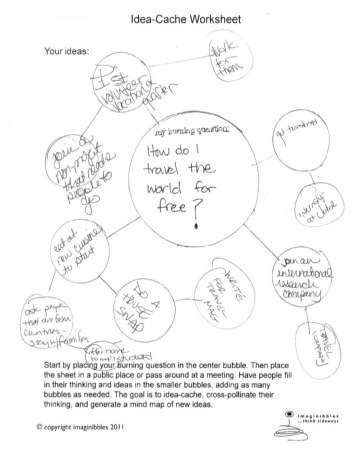

(handwritten notes in bubbles)

- Work for them
- 1st steer volunteer vacation quarter
- join a non-profit that helps people go
- get transferred
- internship at United
- eat at new cuisines to start
- my burning question: How do I travel the world for free?
- write for travel mag
- do a house swap
- join an international research company
- travel company
- ask people that are from countries - stay w/families
- offer name to int'l student

Start by placing your burning question in the center bubble. Then place the sheet in a public place or pass around at a meeting. Have people fill in their thinking and ideas in the smaller bubbles, adding as many bubbles as needed. The goal is to idea-cache, cross-pollinate their thinking, and generate a mind map of new ideas.

imaginibbles
...think sideways

a game-changing playbook for disruptive thinking

Pull-Apart

Sometimes the best way to solve a problem is to take it apart and then put it back together. When you rearrange something it takes on a new shape.

In Cambridge, England there is something called The Mathematical Bridge. The myth around this bridge says that many generations ago, students put this bridge together without nails, bolts, or any other type of fasteners. It was a perfectly formed, well-used bridge. Then, a group of math students decided they would pull it apart and put it back together again. To everyone's surprise, the group of brilliant math students couldn't figure out how to reassemble the bridge without nails or bolts. No matter how hard they tried, it didn't work. Eventually the students had to pull out the tools and add some bolts. If you go punting on the Cam you'll go directly under the bridge (don't forget your Pimm's and Lemonade).

I tell this story because, even though it is a myth, it high-lights an important point. When you pull something apart you see the pieces of the whole very differently and things rarely come back together in the same way. In fact, like the students, you often find new challenges, and when you work off the new challenges you find new solutions. Doing so may inspire new trains of thought, hence new ideas.

Here is a trick I've used to pull something apart. I created this sheet to help me do it. On a piece of paper like this one with blocks drawn in, write out whatever it is you are working on. Be elaborate and detailed and make sure you fill up the entire page. Then take a pair of scissors and cut the piece of paper into blocks, using the lines as your guide.

Randomly select one of the blocks to work on. Tape that block of text to the center of a blank page. Mind-map off it. If you are with a group, have each person work off a different block. If you are working solo, randomly go through all the blocks of text until you've mind-mapped off of all of them.

  Mind mapping is the physical form of the imagination on an exploration

You know the drill—follow the QR Code for this worksheet.

www.imaginibbles.com/think-sideways-playbook/

a game-changing playbook for disruptive thinking

148

First...

© copyright imaginibbles 2011

Think Sideways

Then…

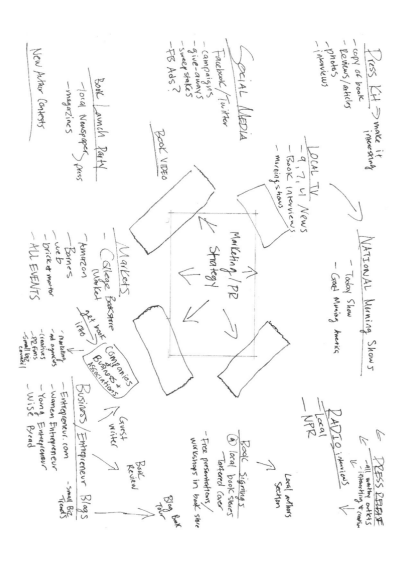

New Author Contests

Book Launch Party
- Local Newspaper → press
- magazines

Press Kit → make it interesting
- copy of book
- Reviews/articles
- photos
- interviews

Social Media
Facebook/Twitter
- campaigns
- give-aways
- sweepstakes
- FB Ads?

Book Video

Local TV
- 9, 7, 4? News
- Book interviews
- mornings shows

Marketing/PR Strategy

Markets
- College Bookstore Market
- Amazon
- Barnes
- web
- brick & mortar
- ALL EVENTS

get book into → Companies Business + Associations
- Marketing
- ad agencies
- creatives
- PR firms
- small biz council

National Morning Shows
- Today Show
- Good Morning America

Radio interviews
- Local
- NPR

Press Release
- all writing outlets
- interesting to media

Book Signings
Ⓐ Local book stores
- Tattered Cover
- Local authors Section

- Free presentations/ workshops in book store

Business/Entrepreneur Blogs
- Entrepreneur.com
- Women Entrepreneur
- Young Entrepreneur
- Wise Bread
- Small Biz Trends

Guest Writer

Book Review

Blog Book Tour

a game-changing playbook for disruptive thinking

Build It

On Tuesday nights in New York City, Saturday mornings in San Francisco, or Thursday evenings in Minneapolis, you'll find a group of people tinkering in a place they call hacker spaces. Together they are working to build outrageous things like a Tron bicycle, 4-D printers, or even rocket ships. They collaborate over a love for innovation, bringing ideas to life. They have created a community and space where anyone can come and take their wild ideas into reality. The people range from software developers to electricians to fashion designers.

Great sideways thinkers are like the folks at the hacker spaces. Leonardo da Vinci and Albert Einstein understood that taking ideas and transforming them into three-dimensional works, no matter how rough, provides you with invaluable perspective and insight. When an idea takes 3-D form you're able to interact with your idea, alter it, and see its true possibilities. Most of us are visual and kinesthetic beings, so having a real object that you can actually touch and feel allows you to engage and see your idea in a more real and tangible way than if it's just a thought in your mind or a doodle on a piece of paper. Whether you know how to build a rocket out of rare earth metals or not, you can certainly make one with duct-tape, paper straws, and an old soda can.

Tim Nicklas is an engineer at The Children's Hospital in Denver. He works in the Center for Gait and Movement Analysis, and has a vision of an innovation center inside the hospital. He came to a public IdeaProject™ where innovators and entrepreneurs came together to collaborate, ideate, and build—it literally came off the page.

Tim built the idea he had for his innovation center out of paper, tape, and a few tongue depressors. In doing so he had some real eye-opening Ah-has. He realized that the workspace needed to not just be collaborative, but also to feel collaborative. Having a room with four walls that you have to enter didn't give off that vibe. He discovered this through his model. So, he tore holes in the wall to represent windows or some type of access. This wasn't something that he had thought about going into the session. He gained clarity after building his idea. Today he is on his way to making this dream a reality, and his business card reads:

Timothy S. Nicklas

Ideator
The Movement Innovation Labs (MIL)
The Children's Hospital

Your idea can be anything—a product, a service, a business, a life goal, a song. It doesn't matter what the idea is. What matters is that you take the time to build it.

a game-changing playbook for disruptive thinking

It's easy to bring your ideas to life. Here are a few easy ways to do just that:

- Buy a bunch of magazines, cut out pictures and words, and create an idea collage.
- Go to a crafts store, buy a little bit of everything, and build.
- Buy a box of building blocks and build your idea.
- Make sure to have tape, glue, colored pens and pencils, duct tape, and some thick construction paper for your base.

When in doubt, buy a kid's arts-and-crafts box and use the materials for your creation.

  Show off your sideways creations on our fb page: http://ow.ly/8vcuk

Wear Creative Armor

There are days where you just don't feel the mojo. Your to-do list is too long, you're exhausted from a long week, or you're under a deadline on a project. Do you know what I do on those days? I wear my creative armor. Creative armor is that one thing that makes me feel creative. It's like your favorite sweatshirt that instantly makes you feel comfortable, except that this time, we're going for creativity instead of comfort. For me, it's a ring and a T-shirt. On any given day you'll find me in a Creativi-tee and a funky ring. Putting on my ring and T-shirt is like putting on my armor. No matter what hits me during the day it bounces off my creative armor.

Creative armor is different for everyone. For some, it's an accessory like a belt or a ring. For others, it's a funky backpack or a sweatshirt. Whatever it is, wear it daily. When you wear your creative armor, you walk through the world like you mean it. You tell others and yourself that you are brimming with ideas.

When I'm speaking on stage I always bring a LEGO man. Every time I question myself I glance over at my LEGO man and instantly get my creative mojo back. It's just a thing.

Buy a Creativi-tee, a ring, a LEGO man, or a pair of socks—some type of armor you can wear. Wearing your creativity equals unleashing your creativity.

a game-changing playbook for disruptive thinking

Sketch

sketch: [a simply or hastily executed drawing or painting, especially a preliminary one, giving the essential features without the details] [a rough design, plan or draft, as of a book] — Dictionary.com

As a child, and even an adult, I spent hours doodling outside the margins and sketching ideas that popped into my head. I'm far from the commercial definition of an artist, but there is something about sketching that brings ideas to life in a way words can't. As the definition from Dictionary.com states, it's a simple representation without the details.

Sketching can be a powerful tool for exploring and generating a wealth of ideas. If you remove the need for perfection, a sketch can act as a starting point to drive new thinking.

You'll find it will take you down a different train of thought. Think how powerful it will be to engage the whole brain in your meeting, discovering a range of thought paths!

Sketching not only let's you engage holistic thinking, it also allows your mind to wander and play with a range of concepts. It helps you investigate the possibilities. Through sketching you can quickly and creatively expand and stretch the mental playing field. I often sketch when I'm trying to come up with multiple iterations of the same idea or explore various solutions to one challenge.

I encourage you to add sketching to your daily practice. No, I'm not asking you to become a showcase artist (although wouldn't that be fun?). When you pull out your notebook, journal, or notepad at a meeting, take a break from the written word and sketch out some of your thoughts.

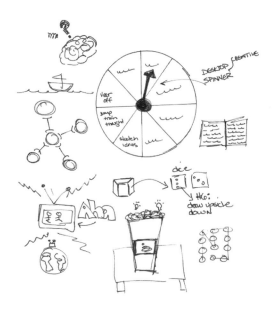

a game-changing playbook for disruptive thinking

So here's my challenge: in your next meeting, ideation session, or even personal journaling, try to sketch out at least half of your thoughts. When you're done, take a look at what you've created.

Did you venture into new ideas? Did you spark new thinking? Did you even have an Ah-ha moment? I think I just had one—OH YA! Here are some tips to help you use sketchy creativity in your practice:

1. White pages: We all know we need to keep a journal. I suggest buyng one without lines so that you have more freedom to sketch.

2. Rainbow of color: Keep a packet of colored pens or pencils on hand at all times. Adding color to your rough sketches can add dimension and depth.

3. No judgment: The beauty of sketching is that it is supposed to be rough and imperfect, so don't put on your judgment hat. Don't worry about your skills, the perfection of the idea, or if someone will see it. None of that matters when you are using sketching to visually bring thinking to life. Perhaps one day your sketches will be in the MOMA, but I'm guessing it will be shown as part of the great innovators of our time!

4. Discipline: Commit to adding sketching to your journaling or note-taking practice. To truly unleash your right brain and reap the benefits of this powerful tool it's important to make this an ongoing part of your practice.

  Share some of your sketchy ideas on fb: http://ow.ly/8vcuk. someone, somewhere will be inspired.

Scavenger Hunt

Many companies ban Facebook, Twitter, and even LinkedIn at work. But I don't think it's social media's fault that employees are bored. Long before social media was around to suck up time, you spent hours playing *Pong, Solitaire,* and *Minesweeper.* Remember those days?

I think companies that ban social media are making a big mistake. It's not that I want my employees to spend the whole day telling their friends they just had a pastrami sandwich for lunch, or uploading self-portraits from a weekend romp, but I do want to give them an avenue for clearing their heads and sparking new ideas.

Do you know how I use Twitter? I use it to chat with all the great people across the globe. I also use it to help me solve problems and spark ideas. If I'm stuck, I'll go to Twitter and do a search for the words "innovation" and "ideation." Somewhere, someone is sending out interesting tweets on those words. One of those tweets might be useful. In fact, while writing this playbook I spent a few minutes searching the hashtag #newideas or #creativeideas and creating the hashtag #thinksideways.

I gained a lot from spending just a few minutes chasing a few rabbit holes. Totally worth my time! It sparked a few ideas for a challenge I was trying to solve.

If you're working on a new product, or trying to start a business, explore words and phrases like #entrepreneur and #smallbusiness. Twitter will yield fruitful results. If you are at work, I encourage you to chase a few rabbit holes on social media outlets like Twitter, Facebook, and YouTube. If you ask me, it's amazing that something totally free could prove to be one of the best resources out there. There's even a new term for it: "crowd sourcing." And yes, check your facts on Wikipedia (LOL!).

Create Space

Meditation was once considered a bizarre ritual for the super hippie; but now, more is understood about the practice of meditation and its benefits. Meditation can be a powerful source for creativity. First, meditation gives your mind a chance to clear the cobwebs and open up the space for creative ideas. Second, it re-energizes the mind and body.

"I have so much to accomplish today that I must meditate for two hours instead of one." – Mahatma Gandhi

Don't worry, you don't have to twist yourself into the Lotus Pose and sit in front of a fireplace for an hour to benefit from meditation. The next time you're stuck in a rut, find a quiet place, set the timer on your phone for five minutes, and just sit quietly without interruption. If you are like me (and I know I am), it's hard to clear the mind. The minute you stop talking, your mind is overtaken by thoughts about your projects, to-dos, and tasks. I found having a mental chant helps keep those unnecessary thoughts at bay. I usually say, "open space, open mind" over and over again. Others focus on their breathing. You'll figure out the right technique for you. What's important is that you clear the mind.

Open space, open mind. Open

a game-changing playbook for disruptive thinking

Shift

World-renowned entertainer and magician David Copperfield, in front of a live audience, made the Statue of Liberty disappear. For years to come people would debate how he did it. He's never officially confirmed or denied any of those rumors, but the general consensus is that he didn't in fact make it disappear. Instead, he shifted the audience's view by a few degrees. The audience was looking directly at the Statue of Liberty, then the curtain went up, and when the curtain dropped the Statue of Liberty appeared to be gone.

How can an entire audience not notice a moving set? It's been stated that the loud noise, music, and open space masked the sensation of movement. Either way, the statue was there one minute and gone the next, all because of a small shift of perspective.

Shifting your perspective by just 2% can provide an entirely new view. It doesn't always take big leaps. Some of the most lasting innovations occurred because of a tiny shift in perspective.

QR Codes, like the ones in this playbook, started as a parts-tracking tool at Toyota. Someone shifted their perspective and recognized the marketing and social media value of these tracking tools. The iPod was a shift on the not-so-easy to use MP3 Player. Get into the habit of shifting your thinking by just a few degrees, and you'll discover a wealth of innovative ideas.

The easiest way to shift your thinking is to shift your body. Sit on the other side of your desk. At a café, sit on the opposite side of the table from where you normally sit.

Use this tool to first get all the obvious ideas on paper. Those are the ideas that come to mind instantly. Write them down in the center. Then challenge yourself to shift your thinking by 2% in other directions.

Use questions like these to help you shift:

What else can I do with this?
How else can I use this?
How else can I see this?

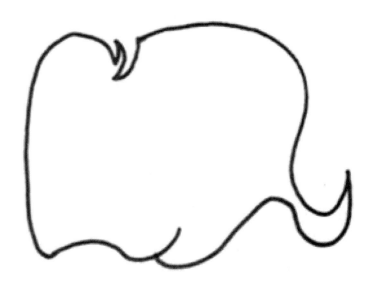

Black Out

Do you remember that game we used to play as kids called telephone? Several people would line up in a row and you would pass along a silly sentence, whispering it from ear to ear until it reached the final person in the chain. That person would say aloud what they had heard and everyone would laugh because it was never the same as the starting sentence.

You would start with something like…

"Peter picked it up to carry to grandma's house but got trapped by a red canary carrying a bratwurst."

Six people later you would end with…

"Peter picked up grandpa and went for red cantaloupe but it got worse."

He he he he he he

Aside from some good laughs, part of what is going on here is imagination in action. Imagination flourishes in the gaps. When it's missing information, the imagination uses its limitless landscape to fill in the blanks. You need to give yourself less information and give your imagination a chance to do its magic.

Sometimes too much information works as handcuffs, because it leaves us with no room to expand.

If you don't have all the information, be thankful. Don't stress about needing to know more. Instead, think of it as a chance to imagine new possibilities.

If you have all the information, grab a pen and start blacking out sections. Take away information. Like the game telephone, create gaps where the imagination can fill in.

All it takes is a thick pen. If you want to go black diamond, try it multiple times, blacking out different bits of information each time. If you are working with someone else, black out information before you hand it to him or her.

> Creative ~~Fridays~~ will ~~become~~ a staple in my ~~work~~ week, ~~allowing me the~~ ~~freedom to~~ travel ~~and~~ explore new ~~territories of~~ thinking and ideas.
>
> ➢ Creativity will BE a staple in MY WEEK, SO I CAN travel, explore AND IMPLEMENT new thinking and ideas!

Feeling really adventurous? Play a game of telephone. Start with your idea and see where it ends up.

Stalk

I freely admit that I am a total stalker. If I think you're doing something innovative, I pay attention. I read your blogs, check your website, watch your YouTube channel, like your Facebook page, and, if you have a webinar, I'll even attend just to see how you're doing it. Stalking innovative people helps me think more innovatively. I learn and grow by their examples. Being surrounded by their ideas helps me elevate my game. Purely by osmosis, you will become more innovative. With stalking, here is what not to do. Don't wait until they publish the story of their lives. I love books and have shelves of them, but if someone is doing something interesting I want to know in real-time what they are doing, and how they're doing it. I will also buy the book, but by the time it's published I've already learned great lessons.

While on their website, watching their videos or reading their press releases, write down three innovative things they're doing right now. Then ask yourself, "What can I learn from what they are doing?" It's the second question that's critical here. You must make the leap from what they are doing to what you can do, based on their example.

Use Your Senses

Sideways thinking flourishes when all your senses are working together. How you see something may be very different than how you hear it. For this exercise I want you to explore all of your senses as part of the creative process. You'll notice that the words you use to describe how a problem might look, versus smell, versus sound, are vastly different. That's a good thing. Each exploration of the senses will take you in a slightly different direction, and when finished you'll have a much more complete picture of the challenge or idea you're working on.

Place whatever you want to work on in the center on the head. Then begin exploring how you might describe what you wrote from the perspective of each sense. Once the exercise is complete, begin writing down all the ideas that come to mind. You know the way this goes. Follow the QR Code for this exercise.

www.imaginibbles.com/think-sideways-playbook/

165

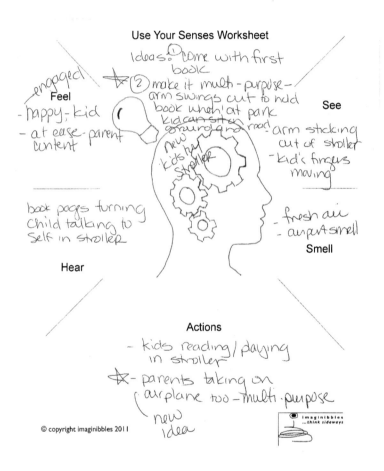

Use Your Senses Worksheet

Ideas: ① come with first book
② make it multi-purpose - arm swings out to hold book when at park kid can sit on ground and read

Feel
engaged
- happy - kid
- at ease - parent
content

new kids stroller

See
arm sticking out of stroller
- kid's fingers moving

Hear
book pages turning
Child talking to Self in stroller

Smell
- fresh air
- airport smell

Actions
- kids reading/playing in stroller
- parents taking on airplane too - multi-purpose
new idea

© copyright imaginibbles 2011

Imaginibbles
...think sideways

a game-changing playbook for disruptive thinking

Look Four Ways

Sometimes traveling in a straight line from A to B is not the fastest path to the best ideas. Sometimes it's better to spread out in all four directions first, to explore how different people or questions change how you might think about the solution.

A client at a major ad agency once told me that this was her favorite exercise because she got to pretend that she was Julia Roberts in *Pretty Woman*. The exercise below has four questions that I've found to work well over the years, but feel free to add your own. Maybe there's a person or direction that inspires you. It's OK to scribble out what I wrote and add your own to the arrow.

Here we go again. Follow the QR Code for the worksheet.

www.imaginibbles.com/think-sideways-playbook/

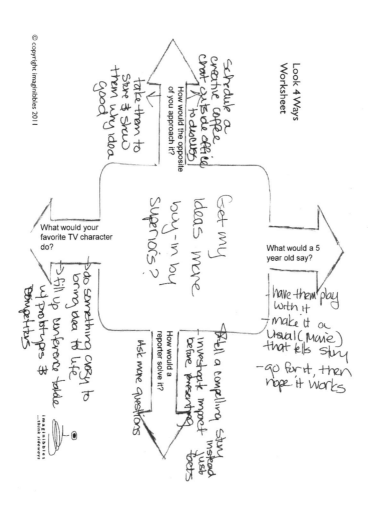

Look 4 Ways
Worksheet

Get my
ideas more
buy-in by
superiors?

How would the opposite of you approach it?

schedule a
creative coffee
chat outside office
to discuss

take them to
store & show
them why idea
good

What would your
favorite TV character
do?

do something crazy to
bring idea to life

fill up conference table
w/ prototypes &
competitors

What would a 5
year old say?

- have them play
with it
- make it a
visual (movie)
that tells story
- go for it, then
hope it works

How would a
reporter solve it?

Ask more questions

tell a compelling story
instead
investigate impact just
before presenting
facts

imaginibbles
...think sideways

a game-changing playbook for disruptive thinking

Depart From the Text

When Will Dean was at Harvard, he yearned for something more than what was being offered in your typical endurance race. According to his website, Toughmudder.com:

> "His David-Goliath vision was to challenge the prevailing notion of endurance 'racing.' He was tired of the incessant emphasis on individual performance, and he yearned for a hard-core event, where completion itself was a badge of honor. The event would demand teamwork and camaraderie in a way that was missing from most other aspects of modern life (including other events)…"

Dean actually entered his idea into a business competition and didn't win because the professor didn't think there were enough customers for his idea. I mean, who would want to participate in a grueling event that tested their limits and created tremendous badge value? Dean and his founding partner, Guy Livingstone, went on to launch Tough Mudder in May of 2009, and it has spread like wildfire across the globe. As of 2010, thousands of tough mudders have run, hauled logs, commando-crawled through ice cold water, and created unparalleled camaraderie with their teammates. I'm actually signed up for my first one in 2012 and can't wait to get my butt kicked. BTW, Harvard now uses Tough Mudder as a "business case study" in their classrooms.

The most unique, disruptive, and own-able opportunities are found when you "depart from the text," not when you play catch up with everyone else. Spend your time departing from instead of adding to the clutter. When Tough Mudder was launched, the world didn't need an endurance race. Instead it needed a concept that challenged the entire endurance category and created a whole new category.

"I told her of all that happened that night – that I stepped out for once and followed my sight. And sometimes it's good that we look for a way to depart from the text and get carried away" – Goodnight Opus, Berkeley Breathed, 1993 Time Warner Book Group. Need to be inspired to be innovative? Go buy Goodnight Opus. It reminds me daily… depart from the text!

Sometimes you don't see the off-the-text opportunities until you take a step back and explore your category more holistically.

You need to ask yourself what you do see (what everyone is doing) and what you don't see (depart from the text). (For hints of finding what you think about those you admire and what they are doing, jump to Stalk).

Once you've done that, the opportunities for new thinking will become evident. This worksheet will help you first identify all the clutter and then identify potential blank space areas off the text. The final step is to explore what your category or idea will look like if you created an idea, business, or product based on the gaps.

The New Economy of Ideas

"Why would I share my ideas? What if someone steals them? And I don't want to give someone else all my good thinking!" — a former colleague in response to an invite to an IdeaProject™ in Denver.

What a shame my colleague even thinks like that. That type of thinking is seriously outdated. There has been a drastic shift in the economy of ideas. In the old days (anything prior to 2008 and the recent great recession), hoarding ideas was a perfectly acceptable and standard practice. Big companies went into their labs and gave projects non-descriptive names like "whirlwind" and "jackpot." Entrepreneurs kept their ideas close to the vest fearing theft, emerging only when the idea was fully baked.

> Be wary. Be secretive.
> Don't share. Be afraid
> someone will steal it.
> Wait until stars are
> in alignment. wait!

But the world has changed and the future belongs to those who embrace sharing and collaboration, not to those who hoard and hide. The New Economy of Ideas is built on a premise of abundance, not scarcity. See, in the old days, people felt that there weren't enough ideas to go around. That is what led to the hoarding of ideas. In total contrast, today is about the abundance of ideas. There are so many great ideas out there that one might say we have an idea surplus.

If you aren't convinced that the new economy of ideas is about sharing, just go to TED.com. TED's mission: Spreading ideas. I'd like to add the word "freely" to their mission statement. People freely share and you can freely watch them online.

TED (which stands for Technology, Entertainment, Design) has expanded beyond its original acronym to "Ideas worth spreading." Proof that we live in an era where sharing is the gold standard. People with extreme expertise on everything from microbiology to technology to education to innovation step onto TED conference stages across the globe and share their wealth of knowledge. It's an honor to speak at a TED conference, and a reward to sit in the audience and listen.

In 2011, I sat in the audience of TEDxMileHigh in Denver and left with pages of notes filled with new ideas. I listened to Libby Birky, who started SAME Café, a nonprofit café where you pay whatever amount you want. You can pay 1¢ or $100 for your meal. Don't have any money? That's OK; you can work in the kitchen instead. As you can imagine, SAME Café feeds many underserved individuals healthy meals and respect. I learned how she did it, the challenges she needed to overcome, and the successes she had along the way. You can bet her lessons were applicable to me and many others in the audience.

Those who want to succeed in our new economy share what they are working on. They open the kimono and share their experiences and lessons.

Sideways Thinkers have known this for a long time, but in the past they were on the fringe. Today, sharing expertise and ideas is the norm. More and more people are recognizing the value they receive from sharing. When you share, you give to the world, you get feedback that helps build your ideas, and you get collaboration that feeds your creative soul.

Still not convinced? Take a look at the rise of co-collaboration spaces. Co-collaboration workspaces are open environments where you can go work for an hour, an afternoon, or a year. They are designed with interaction and innovation in mind. Artists have been doing this for years, sharing studio spaces and surrounding themselves with like-minded creatives.

As with an artists' studio, co-collaboration workspaces often forgo traditional offices with walls for an open-desk setting. Instead of one main conference room, they have multiple areas for sitting and talking with each other. The benefits of working here aren't just the Wi-Fi and printers. The resources go far beyond software—they're human resources too. It's the collaboration with like-minded entrepreneurs. Co-collaboration spaces are open and inviting, and they reflect the entrepreneur's desire and need to discuss, bounce ideas off others, and connect.

According to the book *Cognitive Surplus* by Clay Shirky, in 2010 more than 100 million volunteer hours went into the evolution of Wikipedia. That's 100 million hours of people filling in content, editing others' content, and willingly sharing knowledge with the world.

Again, it's the new economy of ideas built on the exchange of thinking. Today, the strongest currency is ideas—the ability to trade, share, and develop them. Sideways thinkers recognize the value of this currency for themselves and others.

Get out there and conquer the world with ideas!

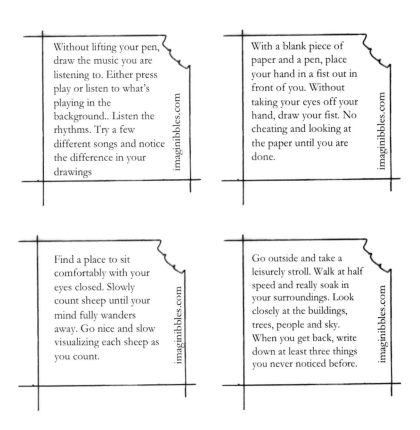

Without lifting your pen, draw the music you are listening to. Either press play or listen to what's playing in the background.. Listen the rhythms. Try a few different songs and notice the difference in your drawings

imaginibbles.com

With a blank piece of paper and a pen, place your hand in a fist out in front of you. Without taking your eyes off your hand, draw your fist. No cheating and looking at the paper until you are done.

imaginibbles.com

Find a place to sit comfortably with your eyes closed. Slowly count sheep until your mind fully wanders away. Go nice and slow visualizing each sheep as you count.

imaginibbles.com

Go outside and take a leisurely stroll. Walk at half speed and really soak in your surroundings. Look closely at the buildings, trees, people and sky. When you get back, write down at least three things you never noticed before.

imaginibbles.com

a game-changing playbook for disruptive thinking

Treat Ideas Like Popcorn

A few years ago, I was overloaded with ideas. It was as if I had Shiny Ball Syndrome. You know, when you can't focus and are distracted by every shiny ball that passes by? The problem wasn't just that I had too many ideas; it was that I couldn't help but pursue every single one of them. I needed to focus, so I did what any logical person would do. I told myself, "No more ideas!!"

That's right, I would focus on working through my to-do lists and shut down any hint of an idea that came my way. I found it difficult at first, but eventually I settled in, and boy did I become productive. I was getting it all done and more. But then something strange happened. I was sitting on the couch thinking about how I could get my products into retail. I needed something that helped me stand out among the millions of other products. I was drawing a blank. I started talking to my right brain.

"Come on, we do this for a living! Why don't you have anything?"

"No answer?"

"Where are you?"

After about five minutes of a one-way conversation with myself, I had a revelation. I had spent the past two months telling myself NOT to come up with ideas. Basically I was telling my right brain, "No thanks, I don't need you." So how could I expect that after a few months of that type of thinking I could suddenly pop my right brain back into gear? I couldn't, and it took a lot of warming up to get it back.

No judgment, no boundaries. Every random idea goes into the bucket. By doing that I'm honoring my right brain's need to create ideas while telling my left brain, "Don't worry, I'm just writing it down. I won't pursue it right now."

At the end of the month I go back and sort through my ideas. Some end up in my business and others go into the files for another time.

Get an imaginibbles Idea Popcorn Bucket for your desk. Your idea-lovin' side will thank you for it.

Find them on our website by following the QR Code.

www.imaginibbles.com/think-sideways-playbook/

a game-changing playbook for disruptive thinking

Playing On The Fringes

There we were. Twenty experts all sitting around the oversized conference room table staring at each other. Between awkward silences we would try to open each other up with the depth of our knowledge. The problem was that we weren't brought into the room to impress each other. We were brought into the room to create a breakthrough make-up product, specifically a new lipstick. For those of you who have shopped the lipstick aisle, you know it's a sea of sameness. Most innovation, at the time of this story, had to do with the release of trendy new colors. We were charged with doing much more than that.

As you can imagine, we didn't get very far. We were coming up with the same ideas all based on the same old way of doing things. Why? Well, for one thing, we were all coming from the same perspective. We were all reading the same reports, doing the same research, and analyzing the same data. With no new perspectives there wasn't much room for expanded thinking.

Also, we were all focused on the same thing, a new make-up product that would disrupt the make-up industry. A very myopic point of view.

After not getting very far, I switched gears and kicked all the experts out of the room. Then, with the remaining team I said, "Let's play on the fringes." I went on to say,

"If we were to look outside of our center, our world, who would we get inspiration from?"

"Not sure what you mean Tamara."

"Well, who does what we do, but not in our category?"

Lots of blank stares until one brave person said, *"Well, lipstick is really a finishing touch on the make-up application, so if I were to think about it that way, I would say car waxes and sealants."*

"Great," I said, and captured his thinking. *"Now, who is on the extreme edge of what we do."*

Another brave soul said, *"I think tattoo parlors and piercing shops. It's not my idea of beauty, but it is on the extreme definition of beauty."*

"Awesome, let's keep going." I said, *"Who else is on the fringe of what we do?"*

Now they were getting the hang of it, and tripping over each other to speak.

"Beauty bars, hair products, lotions."

"Finally, without the hype, what does make-up do and who else does it?"

"Ah-ha, we provide a confidence shield, like designer clothing."

"Now that we're out on the fringes, what can we learn from each of the examples you mentioned above?"

"Lipstick needs to do more than just color. Lipstick can be playful. Lipstick needs to incorporate the cap into the overall design. Lipstick needs to be long lasting."

a game-changing playbook for disruptive thinking

Armed with this type of thinking, the disruption couldn't be stopped. Quickly the team went from obvious lipstick ideas to a lip pencil with moisture. The cap clicked onto the bottom so you never lose it, and inside the cap was an extra moisture sealant so that your lips never dry out, and you could seal in your color over and over again. At that time, every other lipstick was a traditional tube with a traditional lipstick inside. This idea stood out.

This story shows us how critical it is to get out of center thinking and how important it is to play on the fringes. When you explore the fringes you expand your thinking. The center is crowded and full of me-too ideas, but the fringes are wide open. For some it's easy to get to the fringes, and for others it takes a little guidance. As you can tell from the lipstick example, getting to the fringes is about the questions you ask to get there.

If you ever find yourself stuck looking at the same place, the same information, and the same ideas, use this worksheet to get unstuck. Simply by answering the questions, you can't help but explore new ideas. The beauty of this exercise is in its simplicity. Somewhere, some business is doing something you can learn from, so go find them on the fringes.

Take a journey with the QR Code for the full-size worksheet.

www.imaginibbles.com/think-sideways-playbook/

Play on the Fringes Worksheet

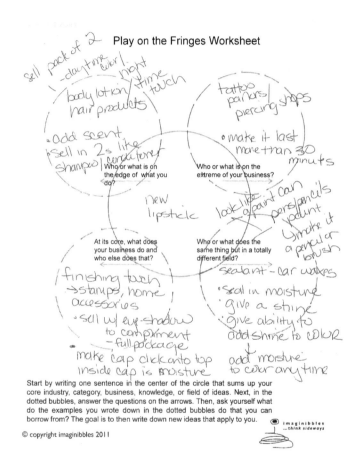

Sell pack of 2
- daytime 'color'
- night time touch

body lotion
hair products

• Add scent
• Sell in 2s like
shampoo|conditioner

Who or what is on
the edge of what you
do?

tattoo parlors/
piercing shops

• make it last
more than 30
minutes

Who or what is on the
extreme of your business?

new
lipstick

look like a paint can

pens/pencils

paint
- make it
a pencil or
brush

At its core, what does
your business do and
who else does that?

Who or what does the
same thing but in a totally
different field?

finishing touch
→ stamps, home
accessories
• sell w/ eye-shadow
to compliment
- full package

make cap click onto top
inside cap is moisture

sealant - car waxes
• seal in moisture
• give a shine
• give ability to
add shine to color

add moisture
to color anytime

Start by writing one sentence in the center of the circle that sums up your
core industry, category, business, knowledge, or field of ideas. Next, in the
dotted bubbles, answer the questions on the arrows. Then, ask yourself what
do the examples you wrote down in the dotted bubbles do that you can
borrow from? The goal is to then write down new ideas that apply to you.

imaginibbles
...think sideways

© copyright imaginibbles 2011

a game-changing playbook for disruptive thinking

Hello, my name is Ben Darules...

I easily break free from the chains of convention. In my opinion, there may be rules but they don't apply to me. I am able to bend or even break the rules to accomplish anything I want. No rule is too powerful for me. I can manipulate anything in a conventional state into something more innovative. You'll soon discover that I have the power to transform how things are done no matter how long they've been in place.

a game-changing playbook for disruptive thinking

Well hello, I'm S.L. Owdown...

I am a super villain and I ooze thick mud everywhere I go, complicating and slowing everything down. You will forget the productive things and get trapped in the minutiae when I'm around. I make it extremely difficult to move anything forward. When you get trapped in my mud you are trapped in the mundane and can't get out. Your legs will feel like molasses and so will your brain.

a game-changing playbook for disruptive thinking

IT'S NO FUN BEING THE ONLY ONE OUTSIDE THE BOX:

CONVINCING SIDEWAYS

www.imaginibbles.com/think-sideways-playbook/

I have the honor of interacting with a lot of different people across the country. Some work in the field of innovation, others are entrepreneurs, and some are college students. Funny thing is that across all types of people I hear the same complaint. I hear people "blame" the other side for not responding well to their ideas. They describe it as feeling like a one-way tennis match where they are constantly serving the ball but no one is on the other side to hit it back. I hear statements like:

"We're being innovative but they keep shutting it down."

"I'm bringing ideas to the table but they are so closed-minded and don't hear them."

"They are risk adverse and I'm not."

Sound familiar? "They" are a tough crowd to please, and clearly never see the value in your wildly brilliant, uncharted-territory thinking. But here is where I'm going to push your buttons. "They" are not the problem. You are.

  "A dream u dream alone is only a dream. A dream u dream together is reality" – John Lennon

It's 2007, and my team and I were about to present our new ideas for baby care to one of the largest baby care brands in the US and abroad. We had spent 6 months doing research, brainstorming, and developing a pipeline of new product ideas. We thought they were brilliant. Our main client thought they were brilliant. So there we stood, behind the podium in the CEO's boardroom.

There was barely any space to move because of the oddly large wood conference table surrounded by plush-but-dated swivel chairs. On the walls were the typical oil paintings of past CEOs. We watched as our client, our client's boss, the boss's boss, and every other person of note walked into the room, ready to be dazzled with the next big multi-million dollar idea. I was sure we had a few, so I couldn't wait to get started. I introduced the team and then stood aside as they presented the ideas, one by one.

To my right I kept hearing whispers. At first I thought nothing of it, but after a few slides of rude whispering I tuned in to listen. I couldn't believe what I was hearing. Mustache man—can't remember his real name, yet I will never forget the *Magnum PI* mustache covering his face—kept leaning into my client and saying things like, "Haven't we tried that before?" "Didn't we see that idea in 1999?" "Wasn't someone working on something similar to that?"

I was getting angry. He was putting down every brilliant idea we had. Yes, maybe it is similar to that one in 1999, but don't you see that times have changed and how we evolved the idea? No, I guess not.

Flying home was the longest plane ride ever. I was so angry at mustache man. What was his problem? It's not my fault he had been at his job for 30 years and couldn't think sideways anymore...or was it? I think I openly cursed mustache man for the next 48 hours, but as I was using inappropriate expletives, I realized something painful. Mustache man wasn't actually the problem...I was.

I didn't stop to get him out of his mundane thinking and into my world of thinking sideways. Of course he was jaded, and yes he had seen it all. As the sideways thinker, it was my job to help him take the journey with me, to get back to thinking sideways.

But I didn't, and because I failed to see that critical piece, the ideas didn't go anywhere but back to the shelf where I'm pretty sure they're still collecting dust.

Had I taken the time upfront to figure out what he needed to get back to a place of leaning in and being open-minded, perhaps the meeting would have gone differently. Perhaps some of those ideas would be on the supermarket shelves today. But they aren't, because I figured the clearly fantastic ideas would stand on their own, and by simply speaking to their merits, I would convince the group of seen-it-all executives that they had their next big-bang idea. It's funny—even today, telling this story makes me a little sad and brings up feelings of regret. But on the flip side, mustache man changed my life and the lives of all who have been inspired to think sideways for the better.

Mustache man, if you're reading this, contact me. I want to say thank you. Thank you for reminding me that as a sideways thinker it's my duty to bring others along for the ride.

You have so many ideas that you just can't help yourself. You have something to say at every meeting. An idea, a thought bubble, a nugget of an idea.

But, it feels like no one is listening to all your wildly inventive ideas that are clearly better than the status quo being bounced around the conference room for the 10th time. Let's face it, those ideas were lame to begin with.

It's no fun being the only one outside the box. It's lonely and frustrating. I challenge you to get over the "they" issue and not only work on being a maverick, but also work on getting others out of their myopic ways. I believe it's your responsibility as the trailblazer to set a path so bright and so inclusive that others can't help but go along for the ride. Watch out for the "they" comments. It might mean you aren't doing your job as a big dreamer.

I was the keynote speaker at an annual conference for the Colorado Hotel and Lodging Association. A lovely young woman named Christa came up to me, clearly wearing her frustration on her sleeve. She told me she loved my speech and that thinking sideways totally spoke to her. She definitely had something else to say so I asked her why she looked so concerned. She went on to share what I would call her life experience as a maverick. She told me how, over and over again, her ideas were shut down before even being considered. She was told they were too weird, too out there, too new. She knew these ideas could produce big results, but no one was listening. It was happening at her current job and had been ever since she could remember, even in her college sorority. If you are a maverick out there reading this book, you know where Christa is coming from. You've felt that shut down. If you are working towards being a maverick, be prepared. It could happen to you.

Unconventional ideas are a fundamental challenge to those with conventional thinking. They are unproven, untried, and have no data to prove their potential. Sideways ideas seem new to the world (even if they are just a tiny shift), which makes them a little scary. The ideas are based on intuition versus fact, gut versus data. We don't always have a direct benchmark to prove their worth.

And as Sideways Thinkers, we jump around trying to share ideas yet we have gaps because our thinking hasn't been fully formed or is a work in progress. New ideas are hard to articulate yet critical to execute. We need new thinking and ideas in everything.

As a maverick myself, this has happened to me dozens, if not hundreds of times. But over time I got really good at getting the buy-in I need to move ideas forward. Her question got me thinking about how I do that. And, how all great mavericks do it…get others to be so passionate that they willingly come along for the ride. So Christa, and all you sideways thinkers out there that feel shut down and out of the conversation, here are some tools to help you bring your ideas to life.

"What I Love About What You Said…"

If you really want to get someone excited about your ideas, give them credit. I'm not saying abdicate your own credit. You came up with it, so you deserve it. I'm saying, show them the link between their thinking and your thinking. Explain your idea by sharing how their comment or email the other day led you to think about this new idea. If you want others to join you and march toward the unconventional, you need to make them a part of the vision. People want to feel important, and explaining how it was their genius point that led you to this idea is a great way to do that.

Some might say this is manipulative, and perhaps sometimes it is. But I think of it more as reaching out with open arms and letting more people be a part of the genius of this brilliant idea that is about to rock their world. I found this tool particularly important when trying to get an idea to fly with my superiors.

If you work in a hierarchical company, this is especially true. In some ways, this tool is more work for you. It means you need to work double time listening and connecting the dots between their conventional thinking and your unconventional ideas. You have to be authentic about your intent to find the value in what they say.

> "Brian, what you said the other day about customers needing to know all the information about insurance on the website got me thinking. What if we had a site that broke out the information in little thought bubbles, and they could click on different ones instead of one long laundry list of information. Given they need to see it all, as you pointed out, maybe we can up their engagement and keep them on the site long enough to read by offering some visually entertaining elements."

A few more starters:

1. What I love about what you said is…
2. What I found interesting about what you said was…
3. What you said about _____ really made me think…

Storytelling

Make it personal. Chances are you've seen one or more of the *Harry Potter* movies. How is it we can suspend belief for two hours, totally immerse ourselves in the story, and come out talking about Harry and Hermione as if they were real people? It's because storytelling fully engages us.

You delve headfirst into a good story. You are willing to suspend disbelief, believe in new constructs of reality, and be teleported to whole new places. New ideas are a lot like imaginative movies. We see bits of ourselves in the characters on the screen. I see a bit of myself in Harry—misunderstood, struggling to figure out my purpose.

In the movie *Chicago* I totally related to the character played by Catherine Zeta Jones. Not because I am anywhere near as attractive as her or as good of a dancer, but boy do I want to be. She spoke to my inner love of dancing and my deep and unresolved desire to be a rock star. Movies and ideas have a lot in common—a good storyline, characters, and scenes that lift it off the page and into our minds. We can personally relate in a way no excel sheet can do.

Paint the picture and weave a story. People don't get emotional (jump to Get Emotional) over data, they fall in love with stories. Remember, the facts and data can be support, not the main point.

Exude Confidence

Nothing sells like confidence. People who speak with passion are hard to ignore and hard not to love. I do a lot of keynote speaking and I've seen lot of speakers. I can tell you that dynamic speakers who own the stage capture their audiences. If you aren't a confident speaker, don't worry, it's a learned skill. Join your local Toastmasters. It's filled with people like you working to improve their speaking abilities. If you feel that you are relatively good and want to improve, I suggest you join an acting class.

Prepare To Be Spontaneous

Sideways ideas often garner a lot of questions. People can't always handle the ambiguity; some because they don't get it, others because they want to get it, and some because they want to shoot holes in it. Regardless of the reason, you need to be prepared to answer questions on the fly.

Don't confuse this piece of advice with knowing all the answers. I know it's hard to believe, but you don't have to know the answers, you just have to be confident and quick on your feet—able to handle it all. To develop this skill I suggest you practice improv. Improv helps you act quickly, respond to teammates, and go with the flow. Improv literally improves your ability to be quick on your feet and adapt to change at a moment's notice. Remember, you want questions. Trust me, a room full of questions is better than a room full of blank stares. If they are asking questions they are at least engaged.

One of the best things I ever did was take improv classes. I'm still not very funny, but I am able to handle question bombardment with ease.

Throw Questions Back

As I hinted in the previous tool, you don't have to know all the answers, but you do need to dig in and find out where the questions are coming from. In my experience as an entrepreneur, working with the Fortune 500, and having to be a salesperson, I learned the hard way that the first question isn't often the real question. I don't think it's that the person asking the question is trying to trick you. I think it's human nature to keep things close to the vest. It happens on more of a subconscious level.

Before answering a question, I might first ask a question back: "That is a great question. What makes you ask?" That one question has helped me uncover the real issues and gain buy-in without having to convince anyone. If nothing else, you get to the heart of the matter and are better able to address their real concerns. The last thing you want is people walking away feeling as if their concerns weren't addressed. The trick is making sure you are you focusing on the right ones.

A few throw back questions might be:

1. "Great question, what makes you say that?"
2. "Interesting, what makes you ask?"
3. "Help me understand why you are asking so I can focus my answer."

If you are unsure how or when to throw the questions back, take a sales class. I know you are thinking that "sales" is a dirty word, but it's my training in sales that helped me launch and grow imaginibbles at a rapid pace. I invested a morning a week and then multiple days in boot camps with SalesLeadership Development and the amazing Colleen Stanley because I understood that my ability to ask those critical questions and sell my ideas was key to success. Trust me, it's money well spent that will be put back in your pocket either in real dollars or recognition and execution at work.

When Words Aren't Enough

One of my favorite stories about convincing is about Art Fry and the Post-it note. Most of you know that Art Fry worked for 3M, and one day in church the idea for the Post-it note came to him. But did you know that 3M did not initially see the value in the Post-it note? They wanted to put it aside and focus on other higher potential ideas. Art Fry didn't agree, but instead of verbally arguing, he gave all the secretaries in the company a stack of Post-it notes. To no surprise, they fell in love with them and starting using them frequently.

Eventually they ran out and went back to Art for more. Art wisely said no. "The Marketing Department says that there's no practical application for this product." At that point, all the administrative assistants went to their bosses and insisted on Post-it notes. It was then that people at the company realized the value in what Art Fry had created.

Art Fry knew that he couldn't convince his colleagues with words, so he took action. There is so much sideways thinking in this story. First, the Post-it note itself, but more importantly how Art Fry convinced his colleagues to buy into his idea.

  Ppl believe what they personally see & feel, not what u tell them.

Take particular note. Sometimes words aren't enough. How can you show someone the potential in your idea? How can you get them to take your idea out for a test drive? How can you show them that they can't live without your idea?

Convince sideways!

a game-changing playbook for disruptive thinking

A CLOSING NOTE

Dear Sideways Thinker -

Wow, you made it. I'm sure you now have a dozen pages, or perhaps a whole doodle-wall, bursting with ideas. Armed with these tools, you will never let a dull moment stay dull, or a dim idea stay dim. Whether your goal is to make a dent in the corporate scene, leave a big footprint in the world, or live your dreams out loud, the world needs more sideways thinkers like you.

I look forward to all the shockingly brilliant, mind-blowing, outrageously disruptive ideas you will put out in the world.

dream big. make a dent
—tamara K

PS—stay inspired (and inspire others) by sharing your sideways thinking with us.

Tamara's Story

Who wrote this playbook anyway? Here is the unabridged version. I have a feeling some of my experiences will sound familiar. As you'll read in my story, we Sideways Thinkers have a tendency to be outliers.

I was born in Ramat Gan, Israel, and grew up all over the Bay Area in California: Berkeley, Piedmont, Lake Tahoe, Sonoma County. My dad is a serial entrepreneur and we followed the businesses. Many people felt moving every four years put me at a disadvantage, but I loved continually reinventing myself. Each move presented me with an opportunity to change.

Not every move was easy, but looking back, I think my parents unintentionally gave me the gift of gab, because every four years I had to quickly make friends. As my parents and sister will willingly tell you, I was a bit of a hellion growing up. I hated structure, rules, or anyone who told me what to do. Let's just say that put me at odds with teachers everywhere. I wasn't a model student.

Somehow, after flailing around in junior college and no thanks to my grades, I got into, and in 1995 graduated from, the University of California Berkeley, with a degree in Psychology— a degree that most friends and colleagues thought was useless in the business world. But it turned out to be a key competitive advantage. While most studied accounting and business theories, I studied human behavior. Knowing human behavior helped me communicate with colleagues and better understand the world of our customers. It probably explains why my first job out of college was at Young and Rubicam, a global advertising agency in New York City. I started as a secretary because, without any connections, it was my only way in the door. I quickly learned that being a secretary was hands down the hardest job out there. I was fortunate enough to have generous bosses who quickly recognized my talents, and I was moved over to the account management side within a year.

After a few years of working on everything from Philip Morris to Chef Boyardee, I decided at the age of 23 that I wanted a bigger piece of the pie, and that advertising was a thing of the past. It's funny how at age 23 I was so emphatic about my beliefs with so little knowledge or experience to back it up. But, I followed my gut (as I usually do) and a friend and I jumped ship and started our own marketing company in New York. We called it The Insights Group. A slightly generic name, but we thought we were being very clever.

Unlike the behemoth ad agency, we decided we would focus our efforts on all the shops that line of the streets of New York City. There were thousands of them, and if they didn't market themselves they would never survive in this cutthroat retail city. We would be their marketing arm, working with them to develop loyalty programs and on-the-street marketing plans before the term "grassroots" was even used in business.

We set up shop in my tiny, no-air-conditioning apartment on the Upper East Side. We pounded the pavement talking to retail owner after retail owner about how we could help them grow their business. We thought our logic was foolproof. Get more customers in the door, keep the customers you have, find more ways to serve your customers. Sounds good right?

Wrong! No one was drinking our Kool-Aid. Owner after owner rejected us. Some were kind enough to give us an hour of their time, but others literally said "NO" before we could even walk across their store. My first real try as an entrepreneur failed miserably. The truth is that most small storeowners in NYC are people passionate about a particular product, and they don't want to own a big business. Second, our generic name and average sales spiel didn't exactly spark confidence. But, like most things in life, it served me well. I learned valuable lessons and it was a stepping-stone to my next adventure.

  Never wrk in an un-airconditioned aprtmnt in NYC in summer & believe n urself before you expects others 2

It got me a job at a very prestigious New York innovation, branding, and design firm, Sterling Brands. I learned so much and traveled the world as a consultant, working with major global brands like Colgate, Unilever, MTV, IBM—I even had the opportunity to live and work in England where I engaged with brands like Nordic Kraft. WOW! But, a couple of years into it I got that itch again. I wanted to build something of my own. The dot-com boom was just underway, and while I wasn't in Silicon Valley, I did feel the pull of the Internet game. I created a concept called Stayingfit.com, a health and fitness motivation and tracking website. It didn't go very far because work was so demanding, but it did feed my need to create for myself.

Soon, along with a colleague, I was recruited to head up the strategic arm of an urban communications firm, a subsidiary of the global ad agency Leo Burnett. At the ripe age of 26 I went to sit at the table with the big dogs. It was an invaluable experience, and it taught me how to hold my own against those with easily 20-plus more years experience than me. It showed me how to use my youth as an advantage. Youth is inherently innovative, so I got the opportunity to become that disruptor.

After helping build that department and develop their revenue streams, I made the first decision of my life that wasn't career driven. I left New York City and moved to Denver, for a boy. I figured if it didn't work out I'd continue west and land back home in California. Fortunately, a husband, two handsome boys, and a dog later, the decision worked out. Many friends thought I was crazy, but I knew deep down that I could do what I wanted, where I wanted. Let's face it—I've never let the safe decision hold me back from taking risks.

In fact, after one of my speaking keynotes on Thinking Sideways, a student came up to me and asked me for advice. She said she had two job offers upon graduation. One was a great job, but in a city she wasn't excited about. The other was in a city she always wanted to live in, but the job had a little less prestige. I'm sure you can guess what kind of advice I gave her. I told her that while I couldn't tell her which job to take, I could tell her to trust her gut and that she was only young once. After 20-plus years in business I have finally come to realize that if you are smart, capable, and innovative you will make your own opportunities anyway.

  Instead of looking for a job, find a way to create ur own opportunities. If u are smart, capable, and proactive u can turn any opportunity into a reality!

When I first moved to Denver I got fat! Please don't say, "No, Tamara, you weren't fat," because I was. Nearly 180-some pounds. After living in New York where you walk everywhere and eat relatively fresh food at every meal, I discovered freeways and fast food. No more walking six miles a day to and from work. No more grabbing fresh sushi and an orange at the local store. It was gas pedals and biggie sizing for me.

When I got engaged, I realized something had to be done. Like most brides-to-be, I did not want to feel self-conscious walking down the aisle. So, I embarked on a fitness plan full of motivation and accountability. This may sound familiar, but my issue wasn't knowing what to do, it was doing it. I got together with some battle buddies and set up check-ins (I couldn't get away with that extra cookie if other people were watching).

With my newfound health, people started calling me and asking me how I did it. They wanted the secret sauce for losing weight. And with that, Bootcamp 360 for Brides was born. We quickly grew to 3 bootcamp sites, 1 in Denver and 2 in California. Because of the accolades for my intense accountability program, I got noticed by a literary agent in Los Angeles, and soon Harper Collins published *Bootcamp360 for Brides*. You can still find it in bookstores and online. (And yes, my embarrassing before and afters are front and center for all to see.) It's actually a great book for anyone looking to get fit. No fads, no hype, just solid fitness advice from someone who knows how hard it is to lose five pounds.

http://ow.ly/8vcTQ

I am very proud of all we accomplished in growing this business. It even landed me a contract with a major motion picture house that bought the option to my story, and multiple conversations with reality TV producers. I sold the business to my employees at its peak and moved on to the next life exploration.

After my entrepreneurial success, I became Vice President of a multi-million dollar innovation and branding firm in Denver called BrandJuice. No surprise, I was miserable. Yes, I applied my entrepreneurial know-how with great clients like Procter & Gamble, General Mills, Clorox, and WhiteWave Foods, but as usual, that inner voice kept gnawing at me.

I loved my work in innovation but I wanted more. I wanted to make a dent in the world, not just give people ideas while sitting in conference rooms filled with bad art.

  If U give a man a fish, he eats 4 a day. If U teach him 2 fish he eats 4 lifetime & drinks lots of beer while he is fishing

So that last part isn't part of the original quote, but I think you knew that. All of my life experiences: the study of human nature, the entrepreneurial failures and successes, moving up the ranks of the corporate ladder, and having kids—they all led to this realization. I was done giving people ideas. I wanted more people to have their own ideas. My life was a roller coaster of taking risks, disrupting the status quo, and challenging myself to dream big. Enter imaginibbles, an organization dedicated to igniting innovation, provoking new ideas, and challenging people to unlock creative potential.

No more fish, but lots of teaching to fish. Whether you engage in this playbook, use our products, wear our apparel, or come to one of our keynotes, you'll leave with more tools for embarking on your own fishing expedition.

  Do u have a sideways story like tamara cause I think you do! Connect & share ur story w/ sideways thinkers on fb: http://ow.ly/8vcuk

a game-changing playbook for disruptive thinking

That is why this playbook is about teaching you to fish and drinking a lot of beer. What do I mean by that? Well, if you know how to fish you'll be catching sideways thinking at every turn, and you'll drink a lot of beer (aka ideas and inspiration) while you're there.

Get your galoshes, fishing pole, and sunglasses ready 'cause it's going to be a wild trip!

PS—if you search your story I bet you'll find sideways cues all over.